Sybil Kenton
'Folly Cottage'
53 West Drive
Harrow Weald
Middx. HA3 6TX
Telephone: 01-954-3817

DESIGN YOUR OWN
MACHINE KNITWEAR

Design Your Own Machine Knitwear

FELICITY MURRAY

W. FOULSHAM & CO. LTD.
LONDON · NEW YORK · TORONTO · CAPE TOWN · SYDNEY

W. Foulsham & Company Limited
Yeovil Road, Slough, Berkshire, SL1 4JH

ISBN 0-572-01346-9

Printed in Spain by Cayfosa. Barcelona.
Dep. Leg. B - 32728-1985
*Photoset by C. R. Barber & Partners (Highlands) Ltd, Fort
William, Scotland*

Photography by Belinda Banks.
Stitch sample photography by John Welburn Associates.
*Fashion garments and accessories, other than those by the
knitwear designers, used in photography are all from a range
at Fenwicks, Bond Street, London W1.*
A special thanks to Jean Litchfield for her technical advice.

CONTENTS

INTRODUCTION

Knitwear is enjoying a fashion boom. Yarns have never been more exciting in colour and texture, and designers are producing some very eye-catching garments on domestic knitting machines.

Machine knitting has become much more interesting and varied and can no longer be accused of being the plain sister to hand knitting. The possibilities on the newest machines are endless. This book shows some of the latest fashionable techniques and creative possibilities of even the most basic of machines, along with the key information needed to start you on the road to designing your own knitwear.

Some of Britain's leading knitwear designers have contributed the patterns and style ideas in this book, and tell of their personal routes to where they are and what they do now.

If you're thinking of buying your first machine the following designs and stitch samples, along with the guide to some of the various machines available, should give you a good idea of the capabilities of the different types of machines with their different gauges (needle size) and attachments. If you're already an addicted machine knitter you will find the information very helpful in deciding on your second (or third!) machine in order to add variety to your knitting.

This book will not tell you how to master your knitting machine – what it offers is inspiration and guidelines to design. If you need instruction, contact the manufacturer of your machine, distributor or agent, who will most probably be able to arrange this for you (see page 86). However, the ideas shown in this book and the patterns provided will enable even a total beginner to make the most of their machine.

APPROACHING DESIGN

Unless you are a fashion design student, it is possible that the very word 'design' makes you slightly uneasy. A design is not necessarily, and in fact rarely is, totally original. So don't try to be or you could be heading for disaster and disappointment. Never be afraid to crib ideas from elsewhere. Everyone does it – including the very top name designers. Even they have to find inspiration from somewhere. It is all a matter of individual interpretation.

If you are knitting for yourself, family or friends, there is even less reason to be afraid of copying all or part of someone else's design. Look at what television personalities are wearing, look in the shops and scour the pages of fashion magazines. You can't possibly come up with any ideas in isolation – you have already taken one step in the right direction by reading this book!

Keep a design notebook and a scrapbook or folder for interesting magazine cuttings or pattern leaflets. Always keep your notebook close at hand and jot down notes about clothes you see – interesting shapes, texture and colour combinations, directions of knitting, details such as openings, trimmings and adornments. No designer tries to keep all the ideas she has in her head until she needs them. If you haven't got the courage to make lengthy scribblings in front of a shop assistant, note them down when you step outside – the crucial information will have escaped you if you wait until you reach home.

Your own individual touch as a 'designer' will be evident when you have finally combined your personal choice of colour, yarns and texture (by stitch pattern or fancy yarn) with perhaps the shape of one garment you had seen with the patterning or detailing of another. The end result will be as original as any 'designer's'.

A simple rule – should there need to be one at all – is *keep it simple*, at first anyway. Do not fall into the amateur designers' trap of trying to put all your ideas into one garment. It takes a great deal of experience and flair to be able to mix complex shapes, patterns and details. To begin with concentrate on knitting an interesting fabric and applying it to a simple, fashionable shape – like the ones we've demonstrated in this book.

WHERE TO BEGIN

In the first part of this book we have concentrated on the ways of producing an interesting 'fabric' by use of colour, texture and patterning. Then in Part 2 we describe the second design stage – the means of shaping and sizing either by basic stitch and row count according to tension, or by charting devices. The principles of Cut and Sew are also described in Chapter 7 on page 80.

The Fabric

THE IMPORTANCE OF SAMPLE SWATCHES

Having decided on the type of garment you want to design, the first step is to experiment with a number of sample swatches to find a pleasing 'fabric'.

This is a most important stage and the key to successful knitting. Walk into any knitwear designer's studio and you'll find boxes and files full to bursting with stitch samples. The walls will be covered in 'ideas' – sketches, cuttings and even more samples – the shelves will be stacked with packs and cones of yarn and the floor scattered with big log baskets brimming with colourful odd-balls.

The time and expense (attractive yarns are not cheap) is well worth it in the end. You can always unravel a stitch sample and start again. Do, however, keep *all* successful samples on file for future reference. Staple each sample to a sheet of paper with a record of the tension setting, patterning details such as needle position/ punchcard etc., plus all the information relating to the yarn or yarns used.

Only when you've produced a sample swatch that you are one hundred per cent happy with, should you begin to calculate your shaping details. See part 2 on page 67.

Sample swatches in the book are designed to show the maximum pattern area and are not necessarily shown the same size as the actual knitting.

YARNS

In response to the great knitwear fashion boom the spinners are producing many beautiful and unusual yarns in striking colours. Unless you have a 'chunky' machine you will of course be restricted in your choice, however there are still some very attractive linens and cottons – plain, slubbed and bouclé, luxurious silks and angoras, and shimmering evening yarns too, in the finer yarns as well as the usual shetlands and wools.

A lubricating spray or wax disc will enable you to feed through the fancy yarns and the less 'elastic' cottons and linens more easily. A woolwinder enables you to prepare 'balled' (or unravelled) yarns ready for use on your machine. Balled yarns intended for hand knitting do not unravel quickly enough for the machine action.

Select your yarns with care. Many a design has been spoilt by a poor quality yarn. The feel of a garment is most important too – a harsh yarn combined with a slightly too tight tension could result in a sweater resembling a cardboard box! Good quality yarns will enhance your design and make the hard work all the more worth while.

TENSION

It is *essential* to check your tension very carefully, as machine knitting patterns are worked by numbers of rows, not measurements. *Always* work a tension sample over about 60 stitches and leave it to rest for at least an hour before measuring it.

Where a particular tension setting is given in the instructions, this is only a guide. This is the setting used by the designer on her particular machine and will not necessarily apply to other machines, so it is really important to find the right setting for your own machine.

Where instructions are given for a particular make of machine, they can generally be adapted to work on other machines; if in doubt, consult the instruction book for your machine. Check especially for lace patterns, as different machines have different ways of working lace and the same punchcard may not be suitable.

In these patterns, instructions for working ribs are for a machine with a ribbing attachment. If you do not have one, you can either work mock ribs – see your instruction book – or work ribs by hand and then transfer the stitches to the machine.

ABBREVIATIONS

When following the garment or sample instructions, please note the following abbreviations:

alt –	*alternate*	st(s) –	*stitches*
beg –	*beginning*	tog –	*together*
cm –	*centimetres*	WP –	*working position*
cont –	*continue*	NWP –	*non working position*
dec –	*decrease*	HP –	*holding position*
foll –	*following*	RC –	*row counter*
inc –	*increase*	TD –	*tension dial*
K –	*knit*	MT –	*main tension*
patt –	*pattern*	RT –	*rib tension*
rem –	*remain*	COR –	*carriage at right*
rep –	*repeat*	COL –	*carriage at left*
sl –	*slip*		

Figures in brackets refer to the larger sizes; where only one figure is given, this applies to all sizes.
Figures in square brackets are worked the number of times stated.

CHAPTER 1
Colour

Choice of colour is of prime importance. A beautifully knitted sweater in an attractive stitch pattern can be totally ruined by the wrong colour combination. Fashions in colour change from season to season, and so knitwear colours must change too to be able to co-ordinate with the rest of our wardrobes. Some colours remain 'classics' but the rest, the 'fashion shades', change with the fashion moods. You will have noticed how the yarn companies change their 'fashion shades' every season but usually continue their 'classics'.

It may seem simple enough to choose a single colour garment to team with the new skirt you've bought, but how would you fare when choosing colours for a fair isle or even a complete range of garments for sale?

To give you some clues, and an insight into how the professionals set about choosing colours, I have asked the *Knitmaster Design Studio* to write this chapter.

MAKE COLOUR WORK FOR YOU

Colour is one of the most important elements in clothing. If you walk down a street, or across a room towards someone, the first thing you notice about them is their overall shape, created by a combination of their body shape and what they are wearing. The second thing that registers, whether consciously or subconsciously, is the colour or colours they are wearing.

Choice of colour can influence the impression you create on other people, and affect your own mood and behaviour. The obvious examples are

black – sexy, red – devilish, white – demure.

One of the easiest ways of dressing is to choose just one colour, and wear either just that, or shades of it. Things become a little more complicated when you begin to mix colours.

There are short cuts you can take to choosing colours. At the beginning of each season, keep an eagle eye on what is happening in the shops, and look at as many magazines as you can. The designers from Knitmaster's studio go to as many fashion shows as possible before each season, as well as making sure they keep track of the predictions for the next two or three seasons. Time spent doing this really is invaluable. Get a feeling for what will be happening during the season by trying to pick out two or three dominant colours. Quite soon you should be able to pick out recurring themes of the season's favourites. Try to separate what you've been looking at into three categories.

1. Neutrals
2. Brights
3. Novelty

You can begin by experimenting with just one to start with. A shade range of about 20 colours should provide what you need. Whichever colour grouping you choose, try to add a new element to it.

Neutrals: try with turquoise or blue.

Brights: use bottle green or dark brown as a base yarn instead of black or white.

Novelty: try navy with mustard and fuschia instead of emerald green or red.

Use these three basic groups as a starting point, and add something you've not tried before to each one.

The next important thing to consider is the area

to be covered by each colour. Dressing in black and white from head to foot will obviously create a strong and dramatic impression. However, things become a bit more complicated when you are covering small areas. Stitch patterns make a big difference to colours. That same black and white will create a totally different impression if knitted in a small bird's-eye check. Using ten different colours to knit an intricate fair isle pattern will cause all the colours to merge and create an overall tone.

From your earlier shop and magazine research, decide which stitch patterns are likely to be popular. Obviously, the choice of stitch pattern will be limited slightly by the type of weather you are expecting. The scale of the stitch pattern will determine to some extent what colours you choose. Using three different stitch pattern cards, knit each one using the colour grouping you have chosen. Choose a large geometric, a small delicate pattern, and an overall subtle pattern. Knit each card in the same combination of colours, then press and finish them. The next thing to do is to stand about two metres away from a mirror and look at what you've knitted, both separately and together. This is how most people will see you, so you should always look at the fabric you've knitted in a mirror.

The more samples you can knit in as many different stitch patterns, the easier things become for you, as you can constantly refer back to them. If you don't want to be guided so rigidly by fashion colours, you can choose a range of colours based on yourself. Consider eye colour, hair colour and skin tones. Unless you have very strongly coloured hair, eye colour is the most important. Go back to your mirror, and make a colour grouping using the range of shades in your eyes. As an example, brown eyes will range in tone from dark browns through to gold. Another pair of brown eyes will range from dark brown to hazel shades. Again, use this as your basic colour palette, and add unusual colours to it. Also, look into the complementary colours of the shades you have chosen.

Divide the colours you have chosen based on your eyes into the three categories we looked at earlier, and go through the process again. Always keep an open mind about colour combinations. A good exercise to try if your imagination is feeling jaded is to take two colours that you've never seen together and try them in each of the three stitch pattern cards mentioned earlier, that is a large geometric, a small delicate pattern, and an overall pattern. Remember, when it comes to something like colour, rules are made to be stretched, and sometimes broken.

COLOUR STITCH SAMPLES BY KNITMASTER

The following are examples of some patterns which can be worked on your electronic machine:

Pattern grid for geometric pattern, sample 1 and 1a.

Pattern grid for geometric pattern, sample 2 and 2a.

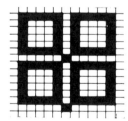

Pattern grid for floral pattern, sample 3.

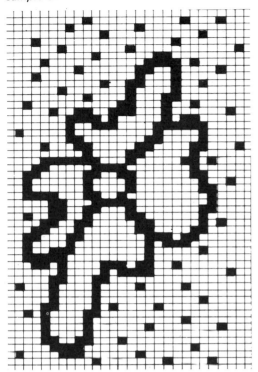

Pattern grid for fair isle pattern, sample 5.

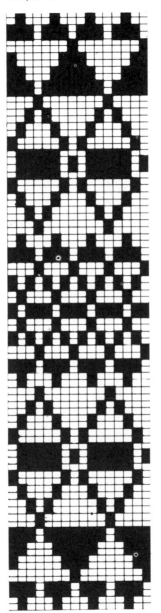

Pattern grid for fair isle pattern, sample 6.

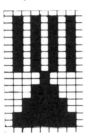

Pattern grid for overall pattern, sample 4.

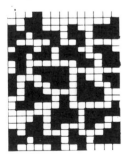

Pattern grid for slip stitch pattern, sample 7.

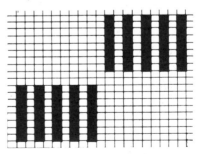

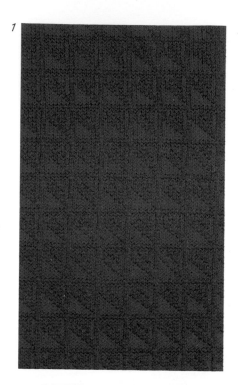

1

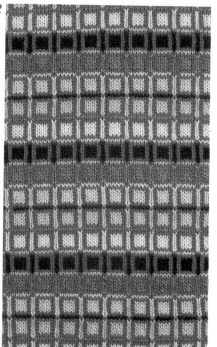

2

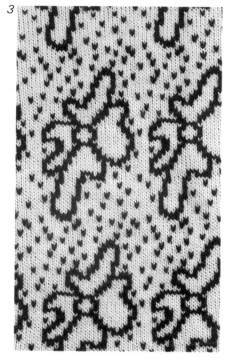

3

1a

2a

4

5

7

1. Geometric pattern in navy and red.
1a. Variation of the same pattern.

2. Geometric pattern in blues and browns.
2a. Variation of the same pattern using black and white.

3. Floral pattern in black and white.

4. All-over pattern in black and white.

5. Slip stitch fair isle using brown and green as base colours with five other colours.

6. Fair isle in navy, mustard and fuchsia, using ruching technique.

7. Fair isle pattern in two colours.
7a. The same pattern using eight colours.

6

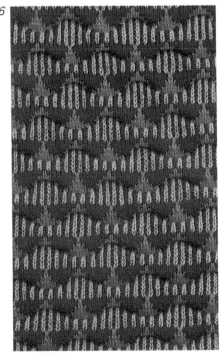

7a

CHAPTER 2

Patterns in Colour

In this chapter we are talking about patterns made in flat colour rather than by stitch variants, that is bold geometrics, pictures, motifs and fair isles.

Basically a different technique has to be used according to the nature and size of pattern required. Over the following pages we demonstrate the five main methods – intarsia, holding, knitting in blocks or panels, and punchcards. Details of using electronic cards are included in Chapter 3.

INTARSIA

Not all machines have an intarsia facility. Check with your instruction book. The Steve Wright sweater which follows was knitted on a Bond which involves a little more manual work than some others. The yarns Steve has used are fairly thick but the basic technique for knitting picture sweaters by intarsia is the same, and the idea could be translated for use on a finer gauge machine requiring finer yarns.

The intarsia technique of knitting is used for knitting pictures, motifs or blocks of colour. The yarn is laid across the needles and not fed through the carriage, and, unlike fair isle, there are no floats on the reverse side. When knitting an intarsia pattern, you usually work from a graph pattern, changing yarn and colour when required.

The needles are pushed forward so that the stitches are behind the *open* latches. This is done manually or automatically according to the machine. Beginning at the same side as the carriage, lay the different yarns across the open latches, according to your pattern. Always make sure that the yarns cross over each other between the needles where the yarns change to avoid a hole between the two colours. Push the needles back into working position, closing the latches over the unknitted yarn, then push the carriage slowly across the needles. This action is done all in one automatically on some machines. Hold the free ends of the yarn while you take the carriage across but without pulling on them or leaving them too loose, or you may find the machine jumps stitches.

When designing a pattern for intarsia it is important to remember that the wrong side is facing you while you knit – so draw your patterns in reverse. Also try not to change colours from one row to the next by more than one stitch at a time. This gives a firmer, neater fabric without loose, untidy floats. Also avoid floats by having a separate ball of yarn for *every* colour change along the row.

Some patterns have small patches or single strands of colour, and you may find it easier to finish these in Swiss darning, as we did with the Steve Wright design.

STEVE WRIGHT

Steve, a talented graphic designer, applies his very individual style (typified in this photograph) to various media. He regards himself as a 'decorator of any surface'.

Steve graduated from Manchester Polytechnic in 1980. He then came to London where, with the help of a Crafts Council grant, he set up his own workshop. Here he screen prints fabrics both for dress designs and interiors. To complement his dress fashions he has ventured into producing equally outrageous accessories – hats and jewellery – knitwear too. But Steve admits he is not really a knitwear designer (as he can't knit!) so much as a fabric designer who applies his ideas to the knitted surface. He sets about this by first drawing the basic garment shapes onto huge sheets of graph paper (this method is explained on page 75), then mapping out the areas of colour and pattern as he pleases. An expert knitter then translates his design into reality.

Steve Wright's designs are always in bright vibrant colours with black and white. He likes the fresh brashness of the 1950s, the bold shapes and splashy colours of primitive African art along with a touch of the Orient. Not satisfied with using anything up to 30 colours in one sweater, Steve will mix textures through stitch (in his hand knits – with the aid of a stitch guide book!) and yarns. In this design he has included matt cotton, shiny ribbon, fluffy mohair, plain wool and bouclé. His clothes are rather like wearable paintings, or collages, at which he also excels. Some of his work has been reproduced as prints and postcards.

Steve's methods of knitwear design are a little haphazard and not recommended for the perfectionist, as an accurate tension (and therefore resultant garment size) is near impossible when using so many very different yarns in an all over graph pattern. The end result is nevertheless exciting and interesting. The yarns need to be skilfully selected with the thinner yarns used double to equal the heavier ones (sometimes mohair works best used double when mixed with a DK yarn) and the shaping kept loose and simple.

Steve Wright sells mainly to personal clients – actresses and people who 'want something different – nothing boring or safe'. He is, however, expanding, and his fashions are now on display in many retail outlets. His ultimate aim, though, is to open his own shops.

INTARSIA SWEATER BY STEVE WRIGHT

Suitable for the Bond or for chunky machines with intarsia facility. Photograph page 17.

MATERIALS: 2 x 50g balls each of Pingouin Coton Naturel 8 fils in yellow (A) and blue (B), 1 ball each in red (C), white (D) and black (E). 1 ball or oddments of each of the following Pingouin yarns: Fil d'Ecosse No 3 in blue (F), Pingofrance in pink (G) ; Mohair 50 in pink (H); Bouclette in peach (J) and yellow (L); Ruban in purple (M) and dark blue (N); Tricotine in pale blue (Q) and red (R).

MEASUREMENTS: To fit 81 to 86cm bust; length 52cm; sleeve seam 29cm.

TENSION: 18 sts and 24 rows to 10cm over st-st.

NOTE: When working pattern, use separate balls for each section of colour and twist yarns where they join on every row to avoid holes.

BACK

Push 85 needles into WP. Using R, cast on and K 8 rows. Drop first and every foll 3rd st and hook up by hand to form 2/1 rib. Cont in st-st, working in pattern from chart and working shaping as shown on chart.

FRONT

Work as given for Back.

RIGHT SLEEVE

Push 40 needles into WP. Using A, cast on and work 8 rows rib as on Back. Continue in st-st, working pattern and shaping as on chart.

LEFT SLEEVE

Work as given for Right Sleeve, but cast on and work rib in J.

NECKBAND

Join right shoulder seam. Pick up 85 sts round neck and put on to machine. Using E, work 8 rows in rib as at beg of Back. Cast off.

TO MAKE UP

Embroider lines, squiggles and dots at random on each piece as required. Press work according to instructions on ball bands. Join left shoulder seam and neckband. Sew in sleeves. Join side and sleeve seams. Press seams.

Pattern grid for intarsia sweater.

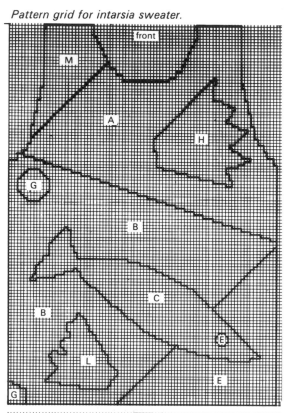

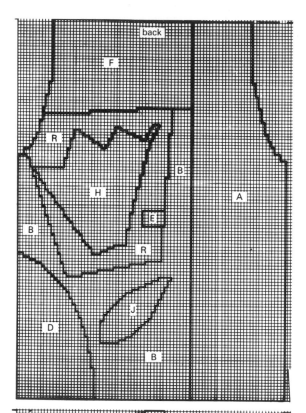

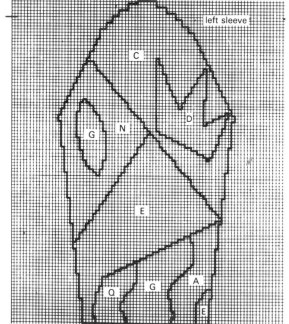

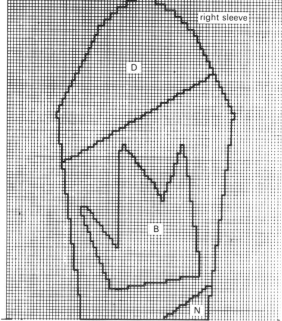

Steve Wright's basic crew-neck sweater design with all-over patterning. Front, back and each sleeve has a different design. It is worked by intarsia from a graph, then embellished with chain stitch embroidery.

Intarsia sweater (measurements in cm).

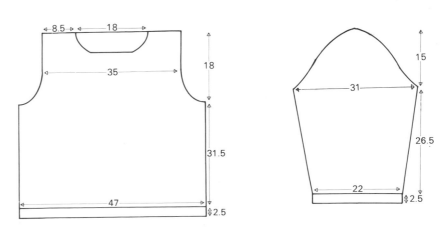

HOLDING AND BLOCKING

The holding technique, which you use for shaping necklines, sleeve heads, shoulders and so on, is also extremely versatile for patterning (several of the designs in this book involve the holding technique). Here we demonstrate how to combine colours on the diagonal. Diamond shapes can be knitted into the fabric without the problem of floats. This is the obvious alternative to intarsia, and many designers prefer it as it is much speedier once you've mastered the technique.

On this bold geometric design, Judy Dodson has combined holding with blocking – that is making the garment in blocks or panels. By so doing she has added variety to her design. She has cleverly alternated small and large diamond shapes by inserting panels knitted from side to side instead of bottom to top. This method overcomes some of the restrictions when designing an all-over geometric pattern on a machine. It also enables you to mix patterns (areas of floral punchcard design with diamonds by holding, for example) and plains more easily. For more about mixing patterns see Chapter 4.

JUDY DODSON

Judy Dodson calls her business Yummy Jummies – which they certainly are. She does not have any particular style that she is recognised for because she is so good at many different techniques. She not only has design flair but a good technical understanding of her machine as well. She can translate other peoples ideas into 'Yummie Jummies' too which makes her very popular with the large spinners and fashion magazines who commission her to supply original garments and written patterns for publication.

Judy invested in her first knitting machine in 1970, and after a training course (given by Jones Bros. at that time) she made up two angora sweaters. She took these to Feathers (a London boutique) and immediately got an order. Filled with panic she quickly advertised for some knitters. She was innundated with calls and it all started from there.

She continued to supply Feathers, Crocodile, and other women's shops, then decided to venture into menswear and got orders from Browns, Joseph, John Michael and a shop in Sweden. She had about 50 knitters kept in constant work plus another 100 on call.

At this time, 1976, a number of shops were closing down and Judy needed financial help to keep her business going. Unfortunately her bank manager didn't approve of women in business, and despite owning a house she could not get a loan. So she disbanded almost all her knitters, passing them on to other designers, and began designing original hand knits for Sirdar and Hayfield. Now she works for most of the large spinners doing machine knits as well, and also directly with magazines. She employs just ten knitters (two of whom are machine knitters) and works from nine to six every day at a studio in her country house. Once a fortnight she takes a day off to visit knitters or clients in London. Judy says she is very lucky to have a 'wonderful husband' who, as he works in London, does most of her deliveries and collections for her.

GEOMETRIC PATTERN SWEATER BY JUDY DODSON

Photograph on page 20.

MATERIALS: 3 × 50g balls of Robin Reward Double Knitting in Silver Smoke (A), 3 balls in Porcelain (B), 5 balls in Blossom (C).

MEASUREMENTS: One size to fit up to 102cm bust; length to shoulders 64cm, sleeve seam 48cm.

TENSION: 24 sts and 34 rows to 10cm over st-st. TD approx 10. RT is approx TD-2.

BACK

Top Panel
Push 18 needles into WP. Using A, cast on, set TD to MT, RC 000. COL. + + With A, K 2 rows.

* Push one needle at opposite end to carriage into HP, K 2 rows. Rep from * until one st remains in WP. Push this needle into HP. * COL. Disconnect RC, take carriage off and replace at right. ** Push one needle next to carriage back into WP; using B, K 2 rows. Push next needle from HP back into WP; using C, K 2 rows. Rep from ** until all needles are back in WP. ** COR. Take carriage off and replace at left. Reconnect RC. + + Rep from + + to + + 4 times more. RC 180. Cast off.

Centre Panel
Push 45 needles into WP. Using B, cast on, set TD to MT, RC 000. K 2 rows. Rep from * to * on Top Panel. Disconnect RC, take carriage off and replace at right. Using C only, rep from ** to ** on Top Panel. Reconnect RC, K 2 rows. COR. Rep from * to * on Top Panel. Disconnect RC, take carriage off and replace at left. Using B only, rep from ** to ** on Top Panel. RC 180. Cast off.

Bottom Panel
Work as for Centre Panel, BUT working first and last sections in stripes of 2 rows A, 2 rows B throughout (instead of B only).

Welt
Push 107 needles into WP. Pick up 107 sts along striped edge of Bottom Panel and place on to needles with wrong side facing. Set TD to MT; using C, K 1 row. Transfer sts for 1/1 rib, set TD to RT and K 25 rows. Cast off.

First Insert
Push 130 needles into WP. Pick up 130 sts along other edge of Bottom Panel and put on to needles with wrong side facing. + Insert punchcard and lock on row 1. Set TD to MT. Using B, K 2 rows. Release punchcard, put A into feeder 2, set for Fair Isle and K 8 rows. Lock punchcard. Break off A. K 2 rows. Using waste yarn, K a few rows and take off machine. + Pick up 130 sts along edge in C of Centre Panel and put on to needles with right side facing. Replace sts of insert with wrong side facing, unravel waste yarn and cast sts off tog.

Second Insert
Push 130 needles into WP. Pick up 130 sts along other edge of Centre Panel and put on to needles with wrong side facing. Work from + to + on First Insert. Pick up 130 sts along striped edge of Top Panel, put on to needles and join as for First Insert. ***

Yoke
Push 130 needles into WP. Pick up 130 sts along other edge of Top Panel and put on to needles with wrong side facing. Set TD to MT, RC 000. Work in stripes of [2 rows B, 2 rows A] to RC 20.

Shape Shoulders
Still working in stripes as before, [push 7 needles at opposite end to carriage into HP, K 1 row] 6 times, [push 9 needles at opposite end to carriage into HP, K 1 row] 4 times. [Push all needles at opposite end to carriage back into WP, K 1 row] twice. Take 39 sts at each end off on to waste yarn. Using C, K 1 row, inc one st at end of row. 53 sts. Transfer sts for 1/1 rib, Set TD to RT and K 10 rows. Cast off.

FRONT
Work as given for Back to ***

Yoke
Pick up sts and set as given for Back. Using B, K 2 rows.
Shape Neck (still working in stripes as on Back Yoke)
Push 73 sts at opposite end to carriage into HP and cont on rem 57 sts. K 1 row. Cast off at beg of next and every alt row 5 sts, 4 sts, 3 sts, 2 sts, then one st 4 times. 39 sts. K 1 row. RC 19.
Shape Shoulder to match Back and take sts off on to waste yarn.
Leave centre 16 needles in HP for neck, push rem 57 needles back into WP and work to match first side.
Push the 16 needles back into WP, pick up 34 sts at one side and 33 sts at other side. Using C, K 1 row. Transfer sts for 1/1 rib, set TD to RT and K 10 rows. Cast off.

SLEEVES
Push 78 needles into WP. Using waste yarn cast on and K a few rows. Insert punchcard and lock on

Judy Dodson's geometric pattern sweater with front and back worked in six strips with 1st, 3rd, and 5th panels (from bottom) worked sideways using the holding technique. 2nd and 4th narrow inserted strips and yoke are worked bottom to top in the usual way – the triangles being patterned by punchcard.

Punchcard for geometric pattern sweater.

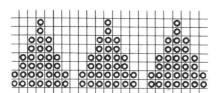

Geometric pattern sweater (measurements in cm).

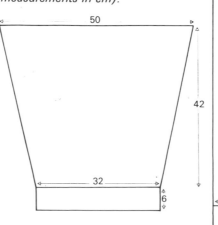

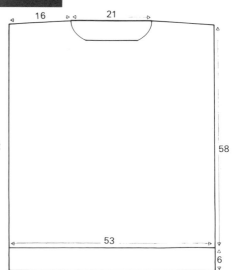

row 1. Set TD to MT, RC 000. Using A, K 38 rows, inc one st at each end of 14th and every foll 6th row. 88 sts. Still inc at each end of every 6th row until there are 120 sts, cont as folls: xx Using B, K 2 rows. Release punchcard, set for Fair Isle, put A in feeder 2 and K 8 rows. Lock punchcard. Using B, K 2 rows. xx Work in stripes of [2 rows C, 2 rows A] to RC 86. Rep from xx to xx. Using C, K to RC 134. Rep from xx to xx. RC 146. Cast off.

Cuff

Push 57 needles into WP. Pick up sts along lower edge of sleeve and put on to needles with wrong side facing, decreasing to 57 sts and unravel waste yarn. Set TD to MT; using C, K 1 row. Transfer sts for 1/1 rib, set TD to RT and K 25 rows. Cast off.

TO MAKE UP

Press work according to instructions on ball band. With right sides tog, replace shoulder sts on to machine and cast sts off tog. Join sides of neckband. Sew in sleeves, placing centre of sleeves to shoulder seams. Join side and sleeve seams. Press seams.

HOLDING AND BLOCKING STITCH SAMPLES BY JUDY DODSON

Robin yarns were used for these samples.

1. Two-Coloured Diamond

This sample has been worked over 44 sts, using 3 colours, A, B and C. Using A, K 2 rows. COR. Push 22 needles at left into HP. K 1 row. [push needle next to carriage into HP. K 2 rows] 21 times. Push rem needle into HP. Break off yarn. Push 22 needles at left back into WP, rejoin yarn at left and K 1 row, then work to match first side. Break off A. All needles are now in HP. Push 2 needles at centre into WP; using B, K 2 rows. [Push one needle at opposite end to carriage back into WP, K 1 row] until all sts are back in WP. Break off B, join in C. [Push one needle on same side as carriage into HP, K 1 row] until all needles are in HP. Break off C. Rejoin A and working on each side separately, [push one needle back into WP, K 2 rows] until all sts and in WP, then rep on the second side. Cast off.

2. Holding Zig-Zags

This sample has been worked in 2 pieces with 27 sts in each piece, using 2 colours, A and B.
For 1st piece, using A, cast on 27 sts. COL. ** K 2 rows. [Push 3 needles at right into HP. K 2 rows] 8 times. Push rem 3 needles into HP. Break off A, take carriage to right, join in B. [Push 3 needles into WP, K 2 rows] 9 times. Break off B, take carriage to left, rejoin A and rep from ** for length required. For 2nd piece, cast on in B and work in the same way, reversing colours, then join the pieces.

If you wish, the pieces can be joined as you knit by hooking one st from 1st piece on to end st of 2nd piece on every alt row, but this is inclined to make a tight seam.

DESIGNING YOUR OWN PUNCHCARDS

Most knitwear designers find that once they have mastered how to design their own punchcards they are well on the way to producing exclusive, exciting and more fashionable garments.

Spots, checks, chevrons, intricate fair isles, flowers, paisleys and squiggles all go in and out of fashion as regularly as clockwork. The punchcards supplied with your machine are probably very basic, some classic perhaps, but on the whole deadly uninteresting. They're fine for getting you started but the fun in knitting begins when you can work out your own patterns.

Vanda Ingham is one of many designers who enjoys most the challenge of punchcard patterning with all the restrictions imposed. Here she explains how she sets about working out her own designs.

Punching Patterns

A packet of plain punchcards and a holepuncher are all that are needed to create your own patterns for knitwear. The time spent designing and making a punchcard is rewarded many times over when it comes to using it on the machine. There is great satisfaction in turning out a complex piece of knitting with relatively little effort. The hard part is designing the punchcard beforehand.

Simple shapes work best. Geometric shapes are ideal. Curves are not particularly easy. You don't have to be good at drawing to design your own punchcards. There are lots of places to find patterns and motifs to use. Children's books are a good source of simply drawn, bold shapes. Cross stitch patterns and traditional fair isle patterns can be adapted. Wallpapers, floor tiles and modern textiles have lots of useful patterns. Once you start looking you will find ideas in the oddest places.

The motif or pattern must fit into a 24 stitch repeat or its equal divisions 8,6,4 and 2 (or whatever number is relevant for your particular machine). Another restriction on most machines is that there can be only two colours in each line.

To work out the pattern it is best to use squared paper which is in the same proportions as stitches to rows in an average knitted piece, that is eight rows and six stitches make a square. This makes reproducing an actual object much easier, but it is less important for abstract patterns. You can use ordinary graph paper but remember that the design will come out shortened on the actual knitting. After working out the design, transfer it to the card and punch it out. A word of caution; if you are using very thick or thin yarns, or thin yarns at a very loose tension, the proportions will be different. Take account of this when drawing the design.

It is unnecessary to punch the whole length of a card if the design fits into less. Keep all the off-cuts no matter how small. They are useful for narrow border patterns, for joining cards together and for trying out new ideas. Cards can be cut up and swapped round and even overlapped to get new patterns.

Geometric and linear patterns work really well on punchcards, except for long vertical lines which tend to gape at the edges; the smoother the yarn the worse this problem can be.

Sample 3 (chevron) shows a simple two-colour pattern that is extremely quick to knit as both yarns remain in their feeders throughout the knitting. The positive and negative effect is simply achieved by swapping the yarns around, and can be very effective when used for different pieces of the same garment.

Names work well on a punchcard but only short names can be used unless you punch the card lengthwise and knit the garment sideways. As you can see from Sample 2 (Kate) there is a two-row gap between each line of names. This speeds up the knitting as the pattern yarn does not have to be removed from the feeder. A four-row gap is feasible without having to remove the pattern yarn, but more than that might cause problems with the yarn getting caught in the brushes. If using two colours avoid odd numbers of rows between lines of pattern as this means that the pattern yarn starts knitting again at the opposite end to where it finished.

The rose patterned cardigan photographed on page 25 uses three colours. The design being in relatively large blocks of colour and knitted on a fairly loose tension, is quite quick and straightforward to knit. To demonstrate how versatile just one punchcard design can be, I have used some glitter in Sample 1 using the same punchcard for an evening look. A more subtle effect can be achieved by either blending a little of your main colour into the rose motif colour/s, or by using just one colour in different textures. For example, a smooth silky yarn which contrasts nicely with a bouclé and/or a hairy yarn. The possibilities are endless.

Traditional fair isle patterns can be updated by using fashionable colours. They are sometimes a little more complex to work out but give a great sense of achievement in the end. I find it easiest to write out the instructions on a piece of paper and use a knitted sample as a double check. It does get easier after doing one or two blocks of pattern.

With all new punchcard designs and particularly the fair isle type, it is worthwhile spending a bit of time on the machine trying out different colours and yarns. The effect of one colour on another can be quite startling. Dark colours make lighter colours look much brighter. Mixed colour yarns can fade into each other. Some quite unexpected colour combinations can look really good together.

The actual design has to be checked to see if the card has been punched correctly. Sometimes it is difficult to predict how the actual knitted pattern will look and a few adjustments might be necessary. The little round or square sticky labels or sellotape that you can buy in packets are ideal for covering unwanted holes in the card.

Multi-coloured patterns can cause a few problems when it comes to shaping, particularly necks and shoulders. If the design is suitable, stop the pattern at the start of the shoulder decreases. This still leaves the problem of the front neck. The cut and sew method overcomes all these problems. (See page 80). There is another method which is very useful for V necks. Decrease the stitches at both neck edges while continuing to knit across the entire front. There are threads left across the V which can be cut and machine stitched or tied. Although I'd recommend you experiment with this tricky method using scrap yarns first.

Patterns have to be matched up at the sides and on the sleeves. A set in sleeve has to match where it joins the body. Sleeves are usually longer than the body so the extra bit of pattern at the beginning of the sleeve has to be worked out beforehand. First calculate how much longer the sleeve is than the body and work out how many extra rows that is. Subtract that number from 60 (or the number of the last row on the punchcard) and that is where to start knitting the sleeve so that it matches the body at the armhole.

Designing your own punchcards puts a very personal stamp on your knitwear. By using the simplest of shapes and one of your own cards you can produce a totally individual garment. It does take a bit of time and effort at the beginning but it's worth it in the end. It doesn't take long to build up a collection of punchcard designs, some of which can be used in a variety of ways. This adds great scope to your knitting. Designing your own punchcards can also be a very economical pastime. You can find all sorts of ways to use up all those odd balls of wool that you can't bear to throw away.

VANDA INGHAM

Vanda runs a small and personal knitting business, 'Knit Knacks', from her cottage in the countryside. She supplies a couple of shops (and for this she employs two knitters and one 'sewer up') but most of her commissions are for one-offs that she knits up herself. 'It may not be the best way to make lots of money from knitting', says Vanda, 'but I get maximum enjoyment – creative pleasure – from it. I could quite happily spend all my time designing and making up.'

Vanda's previous career bears no relation whatsoever to either designing or knitting. She worked in various hospital laboratories ending up with eight years in the kidney transplant unit at Guy's Hospital in London. During that time she took an Open University degree in the sciences.

However Vanda had always had an interest in the crafts (painting, pottery and knitting) and when commuting to London every day finally wore her down, she packed it all in for a knitting machine, peace and quiet, and time for what she enjoyed doing most.

After lessons with Peggy Rhodes at Toyota (Vanda bought herself a Toyota 787 with ribber), Vanda set about knitting all their Christmas presents that year. (Her father almost got a sweater with one arm longer than the other – the knit tracer was faulty!) This followed with a couple of commissions from friends and from then on the orders piled in – more than she could cope with. There were a few sleepless nights at first, but two years and 200 sweaters later, her confidence and experience had increased, and things were less hazardous. Says Vanda, 'Machine knitting is finding new mistakes to make!'

Vanda believes it is important not to underprice your work. Her prices are fairly high, but not as high as an exclusive design in one of London's West End shops. Employing knitters takes a considerable amount of organisation – delivering, collecting, writing clear instructions, payments, and so on. Although there are agencies and knitting groups in some areas who can help alleviate many problems – in particular ensuring there is always someone to take over should a knitter fall ill so that deadlines can be kept. Unless a designer receives large orders for one particular design, it is not worthwhile. For this reason Vanda prefers to knit individual 'craft' sweaters for personal clients. She'd like to start combining more crafts into her designs, for example, inlays or panels of lace, appliqué with quilting and embroidery – the possibilities are 'mind-blowing', she says.

ROSE PATTERNED CARDIGAN BY VANDA INGHAM

MATERIALS: 4 (4, 5) 50g balls of Phildar Anouchka in navy (M), 2 balls each in white (A) and pink (B).

MEASUREMENTS: to fit 81 (89, 97) cm Bust; length to shoulders 53 (57, 61) cm; sleeve seam 42 (44, 46) cm.

TENSION: 28 sts and 28 rows to 10cm over patt. TD approx 9. RT is approx MT-4.

BACK
Push 129 (141, 153) needles into WP for 1/1 rib. Using M, cast on, set TD to RT and K 36 rows. COR. Transfer sts to main bed. Insert punchcard and lock on row 1. Set TD to MT, RC 000. K 2 rows. Release punchcard and set machine for Fair Isle. ** With M in feeder 1 throughout, K 15 rows with A in feeder 2, 15 rows with B, 15 rows with A, 15 rows with B. Rep these 60 rows throughout. Cont to RC 78 (84, 90).

Shape Armholes
Keeping patt correct throughout, cast off 9 sts at beg of next 2 rows, 4 sts at beg of next 4 rows, then 2 sts at beg of next 6 (8, 10) rows. 83 (91, 99) sts. Cont to RC 128 (140, 152).

Shape Shoulders
[Push 6 (6, 7) needles at opposite end to carriage into HP, K 1 row] 6 times. [Push 5 (7, 6) needles at opposite end to carriage into HP, K 1 row] twice. Push all needles back into WP. Using waste yarn, K a few rows and take off machine.

LEFT FRONT
Push 63 (69, 75) needles into WP for 1/1 rib and work as given for back to RC 78 (84, 90), then K one more row. COL.

Shape Armhole
Cast off 9 sts at beg of next row, 4 sts at beg of foll 2 alt rows, then dec one st at beg of foll 3 (4, 5) alt rows. 40 (44, 48) sts. Cont without shaping to RC 118 (128, 138). COR.

Shape Neck
Cast off 10 sts at beg of next row, then dec one st at neck edge on next 7 (9, 11) rows. K 2 rows. 23 (25, 27) sts. RC 128 (140, 152).

Shape Shoulders
[Push 6 (6, 7) needles at left into HP, K 2 rows] 3

*Vanda Ingham's simple
cardigan with all-over
repeat punchcard
patterning.*

*Rose patterned cardigan
(measurements in cm).*

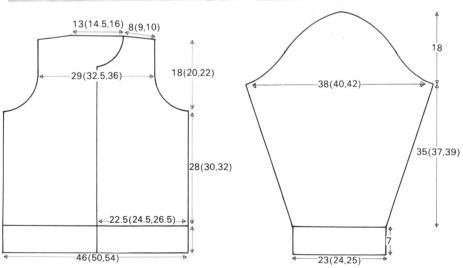

13(14.5,16) 8(9,10)

29(32.5,36)   18(20,22)

28(30,32)

22.5(24.5,26.5)

46(50,54)

18

38(40,42)

35(37,39)

7

23(24,25)

times. Push all needles back into WP. Using waste yarn K a few rows and take off machine.

RIGHT FRONT
Work to match left front, reversing all shaping.

SLEEVES
Push 61 (65, 69) needles into WP for 1/1 rib and work as given for Back to **, but locking punchcard on row 46. Starting with 46th row of patt, cont in patt as on Back, inc one st at each end of 3rd and every foll 4th row until there are 107 (113, 119) sts, then cont without shaping to RC 94 (100, 106).

Shape Top
Cast off 9 sts at beg of next 2 rows. Dec one st at each end of every 3rd row until 75 (81, 87) sts rem, then at each end of every alt row until 63 (69, 75) sts rem. Dec one st at each end of next 16 rows. Cast off rem 31 (37, 43) sts.

FRONT BANDS
Push 102 (112, 122) needles into WP. With wrong side of work facing pick up 102 (112, 122) sts evenly along front edge and put on to needles. Set TD to MT-2. Using M, K 9 rows. Transfer every 4th st to the next needle, leaving empty needles in WP, set TD to MT and K 1 row. Set TD to MT-2, K 9 rows. Cast off.

NECKBAND
With right sides tog, place sts of left back and left front shoulder on to machine and unravel waste yarn. Using M, cast the sts off tog. Rep for right shoulder. Fold front bands in half to inside and sl st. Push 104 (110, 116) needles into WP. With wrong side of work facing pick up 104 (110, 116) sts evenly round neck, including back neck sts on waste yarn and put on to needles. Unravel waste yarn. Work as for Front Bands.

TO MAKE UP
Do not press. Sew in sleeves, gathering top to fit. Join side and sleeve seams. Fold neckband in half to inside and sl st.

Punchcard for rose patterned cardigan.

PUNCHCARD DESIGN SAMPLES BY VANDA INGHAM

Phildar yarns were used for these samples.

1. Rose Patterned Sample
This uses the same punchcard as the Rose patterned cardigan, using a Lurex yarn for the leaves and different colours for the roses.

Punchcard for alphabet sample 2.

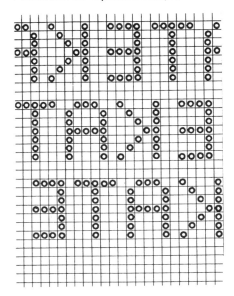

Punchcard for fair isle border sample 4.

Punchcard for jacquard sample 1.

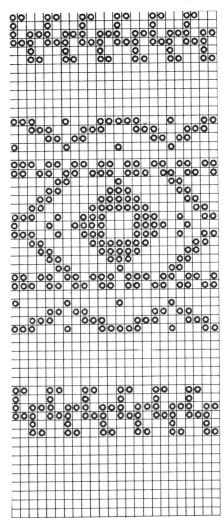

Punchcard for random chevron sample 3.

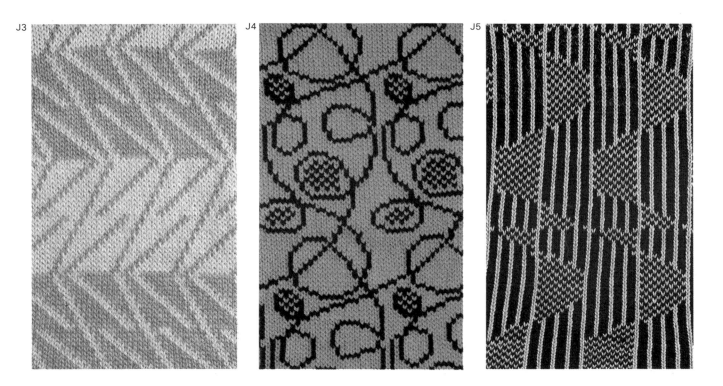

J3 J4 J5

2. Alphabet Sample

This is a simple two-colour pattern and can be adapted to other names. However, you will need to use a short name, or it will not fit into the punchcard, which covers 24 sts. And remember when punching the card, to do it from the wrong side, so that the name will appear back to front on the right side of the card (wrong side of knitting).

3. Random Chevron Sample

This is another simple two-colour pattern, but the colours have been reversed halfway up the card. It could also be varied by using yarns of different textures in each feeder.

4. Fair Isle Border

This sample uses 6 colours, A, B, C, D, E, and F. Using A, cast on and K a few rows. For all the following rows, the first colour mentioned goes in feeder 1 and the second colour in feeder 2. K 6 rows A/B, 6 rows A only, 4 rows A/C, 1 row A only, 2 rows D/E, 4 rows D/F, 3 rows E/F, 4 rows D/F, 2 rows D/E, 1 row A only, 4 rows A/C, 6 rows A only, 6 rows A/B.

JACQUARD SAMPLES BY BETTY BARNDEN

These interesting abstract patterns are all designed by Betty Barnden using a 24-stitch repeat punchcard and two colours only.

Betty particularly enjoys the challenge of creating a jacquard pattern that doesn't look as though it repeats. She plans her designs on large sheets of ordinary graph paper, drawing each design repeated at least four times to gauge the final result as best she can (drawing, she says, long and thin and trying to imagine how it'll look shorter and fatter!).

Note that Sample 3 uses punchcard B from the ruched Sample 5 on page 46–7.

Punchcard for jacquard sample 2. *Punchcard for jacquard sample 4.* *Punchcard for jacquard sample 5.*

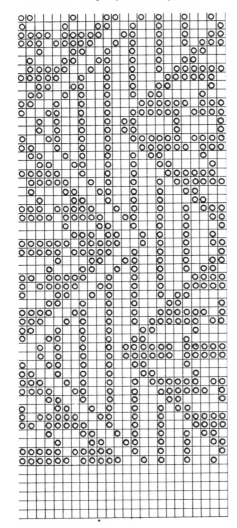 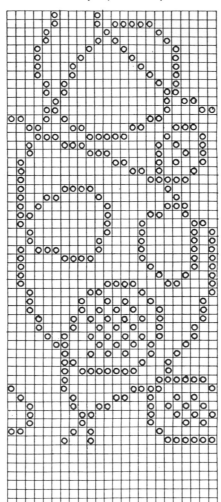 

CHAPTER 3

Patterning with an Electronic Machine

The patterning possibilities of the latest electronic machines are almost mind-blowing! There are no limitations on the size of the repeat as with a punchcard, and the pattern, or motif, can be mirror repeated too. Some machines can also take up to four colour changes in a single row. These machines are a designer's dream, and to explain how to set about making the most of the versatility of their patterning systems, I have asked the experts at *The Knitmaster Design Studio*.

DESIGNING ON ELECTRONIC MACHINES

The last few years have seen quite a revolution in machine knitting, particularly since Knitmaster introduced the first ever electronic knitting machine.

Each aspect of electronic knitting attracts its own fans. The most quoted reasons for choosing an electronic rather than a punchcard machine are as follows:

1. With transparent, blank design cards, it's very quick and easy to draw straight onto the card, rather than work out a pattern on graph paper, transfer it to a blank card, and punch out the card. If you make a mistake, or want to alter part of the pattern, you simply rub it out, instead of sticking sellotape all over the place.

2. Designing or working out a pattern is much quicker on an electronic machine because you only need to draw one section of a pattern, and the machine takes care of repeating it both lengthways and widthways.

3. As you can rub out, the blank design cards are re-usable, so you don't have to keep buying packs of new punchcards.

These basic differences are just the beginning of the electronic story. All the push buttons on the machine vary the basic pattern you start with. I've found there are two different ways to approach designing using an electronic machine. The first way is to start with a fairly simple, small pattern and use the facilities of the machine to make it more interesting. Use the push buttons to alter the basic design, and try using the buttons in different combinations. Use the point cams to move the pattern about on the knitting. With the point cams, you can position the pattern area anywhere you like on a garment – you don't have to work over specific groups of needles. Build up a larger shape by moving the point cams, with the basic pattern repeating within the larger shape.

The second way to start designing with an electronic machine is to begin with a large, intricate motif. Use this as the main point of interest on a garment, then select areas for trims, borders and so on. Isolate stitch areas by using the pattern width indicator. Use the mirror repeat button on this smaller area. Isolate row sections by resetting the row repeat column. Knit the pattern upside down, then the right way up by using the change of direction button. An easy motif to start with is a right-angled triangle drawn in the left corner of the card, or a quarter circle. Motifs on knitting can look a little square-shaped, and starting with a triangle or a quarter circle gives you a new look right from the start.

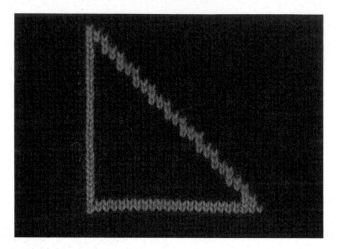

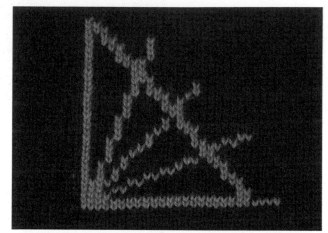

Beginning with this basic shape, start to put pattern inside it. The cobweb pattern on the electronic dress started as a quarter circle, with straight lines radiating from the right angle at the bottom left of the card. The whole cobweb was made by knitting from the top of the card to the bottom, using the double-the-length button, and the mirror repeat button. The top half of the pattern was knitted from the bottom to the top of the card, using the mirror repeat button. The fair isle borders were knitted using sections of the card, both with and without the mirror repeat button. You can see how the character of the original motif has been changed by doing this. Try both these starting points (a small simple pattern, and a large motif) for yourself, and then start experimenting using the following guidelines.

Any pattern you draw should be the beginning, not the end of designing. Start with a rough idea of what you're trying to achieve, then draw it out on the card. Knit through the pattern several times – enough to make sure it repeats if you want to use it as an all-over pattern. Try it as a motif, and with all possible variations. Always use every facility the machine has to offer – you can be surprised by the result. Use all the push buttons, move the pattern width indicator, knit the card from top to bottom and back again. Try all your ideas on one length of fabric, then cut them up, and combine two or three different samples. Always look at samples in a

'Cobweb' dress showing expanded and mirror repeat patterning possible on electronic card machine.

mirror – you'll get a much clearer sight of them that way. The final stage is to think about adding to the knitting. Would appliqué, quilting, beading or threading improve or detract from the design?

When you're planning a garment, don't knit the first thing you think of. Write out a checklist of all the features of your machine. Each time you design a new pattern, go through the list and think about how it would look with that variation. Try a sample of anything you think might work. Always keep an open mind about what you are knitting. Keep all your samples for future reference, and remember – enjoy yourself.

COBWEB DRESS BY KNITMASTER

These instructions are for Knitmaster SK560 Electronic Machine with KR7 Knitradar and garter bar.

Draw your Knitradar pattern for this dress using the measurements shown on the diagram. The diagram is shown in one size to fit 91cm bust, but you can make it larger or smaller, longer or shorter as you wish. If you don't have the full width KR7 Knitradar, you should draw only half the pattern.

MATERIALS: Of Knitmaster Kone 4ply, 460g in Black (A), 15g in Opal (B), 10g in Matador (C), 10g

Different stages of the cobweb pattern.

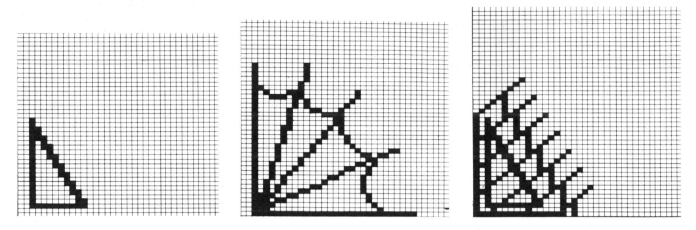

Cobweb dress (measurements in cm).

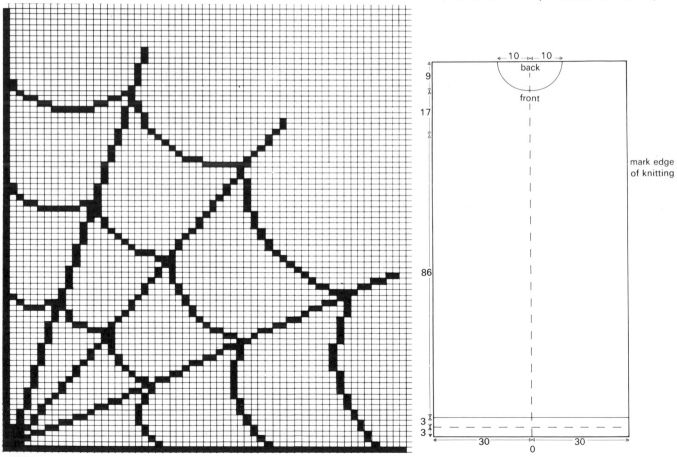

in Fashion Flip (D), 35g in Saxe Blue (E) and 10g in Lilac lurex type yarn (F).

MEASUREMENT: To fit 86 to 91cm bust; length 116cm; sleeve seam 44cm.

TENSION: 32 sts and 44 rows to 10cm over st st. TD approx 6. 32 sts and 41 rows to 10cm over Fair Isle. TD approx 6.

PATTERNS: Use special card.

Pattern 1
K 2 rows F, 1 row A.
Set card to row 1; pattern width indicator 26; point cams width of knitting; needle 1 cam 26 and 27 at right of 0; buttons 1 (left), 2 (left) and 5.
With A in feeder 1 and B in feeder 2, K in Fair Isle until 2nd buzzer, then K 1 more row Fair Isle and 1 row A.

Pattern 2
K 2 rows F, 1 row A.
Set card to row 1; pattern width indicator 26; point cams width of knitting; needle 1 cam 13 and 14 at right of 0; buttons 1 (left) and 2 (left) only.
With A in feeder 1 and C in feeder 2, K in Fair Isle until 2nd buzzer, then K 1 more row Fair Isle and 1 row A.

Pattern 3
K 2 rows F, 1 row A.
Set card to row 1; pattern width indicator 16; point cams width of knitting; needle 1 cam 16 and 17 at right of 0; buttons 1 (left) and 2 (left) only.
With A in feeder 1 and D in feeder 2, K in Fair Isle until 1st buzzer, then K 1 more row Fair Isle and 1 row A.

Pattern 4
Set card to row 1; pattern width indicator 26; point cams 26 left and right of 0; needle 1 cam 26 and 27 at right of 0; buttons 1 (left), 2 (left) and 5.
With A in feeder 1 and E in feeder 2, K in Fair Isle until 2nd buzzer, then K 1 more row Fair Isle. Return card to row 1. K 1 row in A. Repeat twice more (8 times more for front).

Pattern 5
K 2 rows A.
Set card to row 82; pattern width indicator 60; point cams 60 left and right of 0; needle 1 cam 60 and 61 at right of 0; buttons 1 (left), 2 (left), 3 and 5; card direction knob with right hand light on. With A in feeder 1 and E in feeder 2, K in Fair Isle. When 4th buzzer sounds, button 3 light off. K until 7th buzzer sounds, then continue in A.

BACK
Using automatic method and A cast on. Set TD to MT-2, K to broken line on radar. Set TD to MT, K 1 row. Set TD to MT-1, K to next line on radar. Pick up a hem. K 2 rows. ** K patterns 1 to 5 as given above, then cont in A until Back is completed.

FRONT
Work as given for Back to ** K patterns 1 to 3 as given above, then K 5 repeats of pattern 4. Cont in A as shown on radar.

SLEEVES
Using automatic method and A cast on. K to broken line. K pattern 3 but omit the 2 rows F and 1 row A. Continue in A as shown on radar.

TO MAKE UP
Pin out to size and press according to instructions on cone. Join shoulder seams. Set in sleeves between marked points. Join side and sleeve seams. Turn in 1cm round neck and sl st. Press seams.

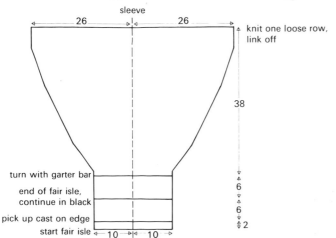

sleeve

26   26

knit one loose row, link off

38

turn with garter bar
end of fair isle, continue in black
pick up cast on edge
start fair isle

6
6
2

10   10

CHAPTER 4

Special Techniques

Once you have become adept at using punchcards and creating your own pattern repeats, there are many ways in which you can enhance these – by ruching, mixing patterns on a garment, adding beads or sequins, pleating – the possibilities are endless.

On the following pages I have selected ideas from three designers to inspire you. Betty Barnden is famed for her ruched effects, Sarah Dallas for her stylish pattern combinations and adornment, and Julia Pines for her classics with a difference this time demonstrating some ways of using pleating and 'holding' techniques.

MIXING PUNCHCARD PATTERNS

SARAH DALLAS

Sarah Dallas is today a successful and internationally known fashion designer, specialising in knitwear teamed with specially woven co-ordinating skirts. She lives and works with her partner and boyfriend, John Bolley. John runs the business and financial side leaving Sarah free to concentrate on design aspects. Their 'head office' and studio is a light and spacious old listed warehouse (fittingly where fleeces were once sorted) in Lancashire. She employs a bookkeeper and two other full-time assistants as well as a hundred knitters to enable her to fulfill her orders. Sarah Dallas designs can be seen in Harrods, Harvey Nichols, Selfridges, Simpsons and other such well known fashion shops in England, Scotland, Eire, France, Italy, Denmark, Germany, Canada, Australia and the USA. Sarah also finds time to teach her pet subject, 'creative' machine knitting, to fashion design students. Sarah has come a long way since starting out on her career in 1970.

Sarah took an art foundation course at the NE London Polytechnic followed by a BA(Hons) degree in Textiles at Middlesex Poly. Finally in 1976 she graduated from the Royal College of Art (Textiles School) and began her own business from her London bedsit. She took her exclusive hand and machine knit designs around the high class London fashion shops and stores until she had sufficient orders to warrant a string of out-workers. Then she moved north. Working day and night from home she gradually built up her business to what it is today. By showing her collections at the fashion trade fairs she has made her name internationally famous.

Sarah Dallas's designs are instantly recognisable – dynamic colour combinations in bold patterns and shapes with the clever mixing of three or more patterns in one garment. But her original 'hallmark' that first got her recognised was her machine knitted lacy designs with intricate hand ribbon and bead work. (See her samples on pages 40–1.)

The paisley/rose/spot pattern sweater design typifies Sarah's current 'hallmark'. She has successfully combined areas of flowers, paisley, spots and plain by the careful use of just four (one main, three secondary) common colours. As a

*'Boxy' sweater with drop
shoulders and front
pockets, showing how
plains and patterns can be
attractively mixed. The
back is the same as the
front, minus pockets, but
note the different sleeves.*

Paisley/rose/spot sweater (measurements in cm).

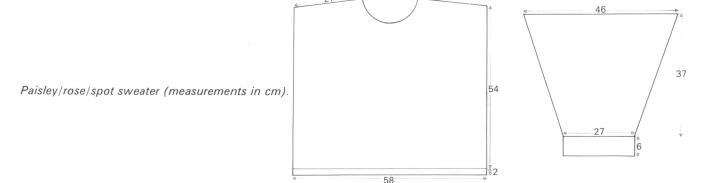

general guide: either the pattern or the colour should be constant for a design to 'hold together'. That is, if you are using a vast number of colours the pattern should flow all over the sweater, and, if you are piecing together several different blocks of patterning, the colours should be constant throughout.

PAISLEY/ROSE/SPOT PATTERN SWEATER BY SARAH DALLAS

Photograph on page 37.

MATERIALS: 6 × 50g balls of Naturally Beautiful Coton Mat in Pink (A), 5 balls in Blue (B), 4 balls in Yellow (C), 1 ball in Green (D).

MEASUREMENTS: to fit 86 to 97cm Bust; length to shoulders 56cm; sleeve seam 43cm.

TENSION: 29 sts and 33 rows to 10cm measured over Paisley or Rose patt; 26 sts and 33 rows to 10cm over Spot patt. TD approx 10. RT is approx MT-3.

BACK

Push 168 needles into WP. Using waste yarn, cast on and K a few rows. COL. Break off waste yarn, join in B. Set TD to 6, K 6 rows, TD 10, K 1 row, TD 6, K 6 rows. Put loops of first row in B on to needles and unravel waste yarn. Insert Rose punchcard and lock on row 1. RC 000. Set TD to MT, K 2 rows. Release punchcard and set machine for Fair Isle. Using B in feeder 1 throughout, K 5 rows with D in feeder 2, then 14 rows with A. Rep these 19 rows once more, then the first 5 of them again. Remove punchcard and K 1 row in B. RC 46. Using C, K 4 rows. Pick up loops from first row in C and put on to needles to form a tuck. ** Insert Paisley punchcard and lock on row 1. Reset RC to 46. Using A, K 2 rows. Release punchcard and set machine for Fair Isle. Using A in feeder 1 throughout, work 12 rows with B in feeder 2, 4 rows with D, 10 rows with C, 4 rows with D. Repeat these 30 rows 3 times more, then the first 10 rows again. RC 178

Shape Shoulders

[Push 15 needles at left into HP, K 1 row; push 15 needles at right into HP, K 1 row] 4 times. (Before working last 2 rows, lock punchcard and cont in A.) Push all needles back into WP. Using waste yarn K a few rows and take off machine.

FRONT

Work as given for Back to **.

Pockets

Push 24 needles at left and 104 needles at right into HP and cont on 40 sts in WP. Using C, K 70 rows. Break off C and push needles into HP. Leaving 24 needles at right and 104 needles at left in HP, push 40 needles into WP and work to match first pocket. Push all needles back into WP. Continue as for Back from ** to RC 152.

Shape Neck

Push 96 needles at left into HP and cont on rem 72 sts. K 2 rows. (Using double transfer tool, dec one st at neck edge, K 2 rows) 12 times, then K 1 row. 60 sts. RC 179.

Shape Shoulder

[Push 15 needles at right into HP, K 2 rows] 3 times. Push all needles back into WP, then using waste yarn, K a few rows and take off machine. Push centre 24 needles back into WP; using waste yarn, K a few rows and take off machine. Push rem 72 needles back into WP and work to match first side.

RIGHT SLEEVE

Push 71 needles into WP for 1/1 rib. Using A, cast on, set TD to RT and K 26 rows. Transfer sts to main bed, inc one st at end of row. 72 sts. COR. Insert Spot punchcard and lock on row 1. Set TD to MT, RC 000. K 2 rows. Release punchcard and set machine for Fair Isle. Using A in feeder 1 and B in feeder 2, cont in patt, inc one st at each end of every 4th row until there are 122 sts, then K to RC 122. Cast off *loosely*.

LEFT SLEEVE

Work as given for Right Sleeve, but using C instead of B.

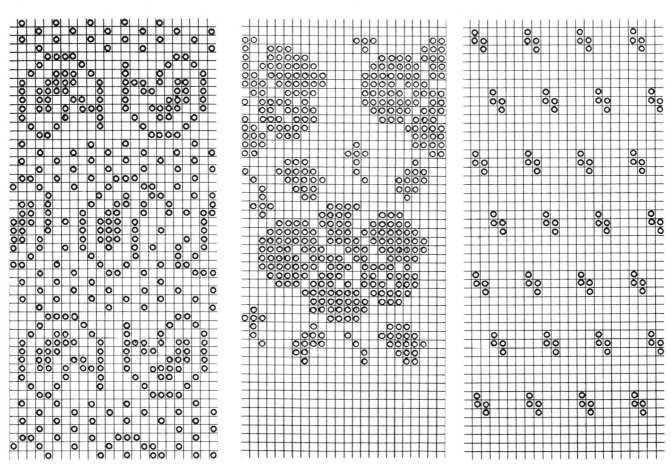

NECKBAND

Join left shoulder seam as folls: push 60 needles into WP. With WRONG side of work facing put left back shoulder sts on to needles, then with RIGHT side facing put sts of left front shoulder on to needles and unravel waste yarn from both pieces. Using C, cast off both sets of sts tog (so that cast off shows on the right side).

Push 103 needles into WP for 1/1 rib. Using A, cast on, set TD to RT and K 10 rows. Transfer sts to main bed.

Pick up 103 sts round neck edge, including sts on waste yarn and put on to needles with wrong side facing. Unravel waste yarn. Using A, cast sts off tog.

TO MAKE UP

Join right shoulder seam as for left and join neckband seam. Press work according to instructions on ball band. Sew in sleeves, placing centre of sleeves to shoulder seams. Join side and sleeve seams. Join sides of pockets. Press seams.

LACY SAMPLES USING RIBBON AND BEADING
BY SARAH DALLAS

All these samples use cotton or silk yarns by Naturally Beautiful.

1. Cable and Chevron Pattern

This pattern uses 2 colours, A and B.
Insert punchcard and lock on row 1. Using A, cast on and K a few rows. Release punchcard and set machine for Fair Isle. With A in feeder 1 and B in feeder 2, K 4 rows. * Using triple transfer tool, make a cable over each group of 6 sts in A. K 8 rows. Rep from * for length reqd. Thread ribbon through cables if required.

2. Fair Isle Pattern with Diamanté

This pattern uses 4 colours, A, B, C and D.
Insert punchcard and lock on row 1. Using A, cast on and K a few rows. Release punchcard and set machine for Fair Isle. With A in feeder 1 throughout, K 4 rows with B in feeder 2, 3 rows with C, 4 rows with B, 1 row in A only, 2 rows with D, 1 row with B, 2 rows with D, 1 row with A only. Rep these 18 rows throughout. When completed, sew on beads, or fix diamanté with applicator.

3. Chevron Lace Pattern with Beads or Diamanté

This is worked on a machine with a lace carriage. The punchcard is for a Jones machine, but can possibly be adapted for others – see instruction manual.
When completed, sew on beads or fix diamanté as required and thread ribbon through holes.

4. 'Fir Trees' Lace Pattern with Beads

See Chevron Lace Pattern above.

5. Diamond Pattern in Tuck Stitch with Beads Knitted In

Before starting, thread beads on to a separate ball of yarn. Insert punchcard and lock on row 1. Cast on and K a few rows. Release punchcard and set machine for Tuck Stitch. K 2 rows. Take yarn with

beads on across from right to left and K the sts by hand, placing one bead behind the tucked sts on every 8th st as shown below:

oovovooooovovooooovovooo
   ↑   ↑   ↑

Do not count this row on RC. K 10 rows.
* K beaded yarn across by hand, this time from left to right, placing beads as below:

oooooovooooooovoooooooov
     ↑   ↑   ↑

Do not count this row on RC. K 12 rows.
K beaded yarn across by hand, this time from right to left, placing beads as below:

ooovoooooovooooooovoooo
   ↑   ↑   ↑

Do not count this row on RC. K 12 rows.
Rep the 24 rows from * as required.
Alternatively, work tuck pattern from the punchcard, then sew on beads afterwards as required.

6 and 6a. Making Holes

Where a hole is required, take a separate length of yarn and cast off the required number of sts by hand, then cast them on again. Continue knitting across all sts until next hole is required.
Alternatively, where a hole is required, knit the required number of sts by hand, using a length of contrast yarn. When work is completed, remove contrast yarn and neaten the sts as for a buttonhole.

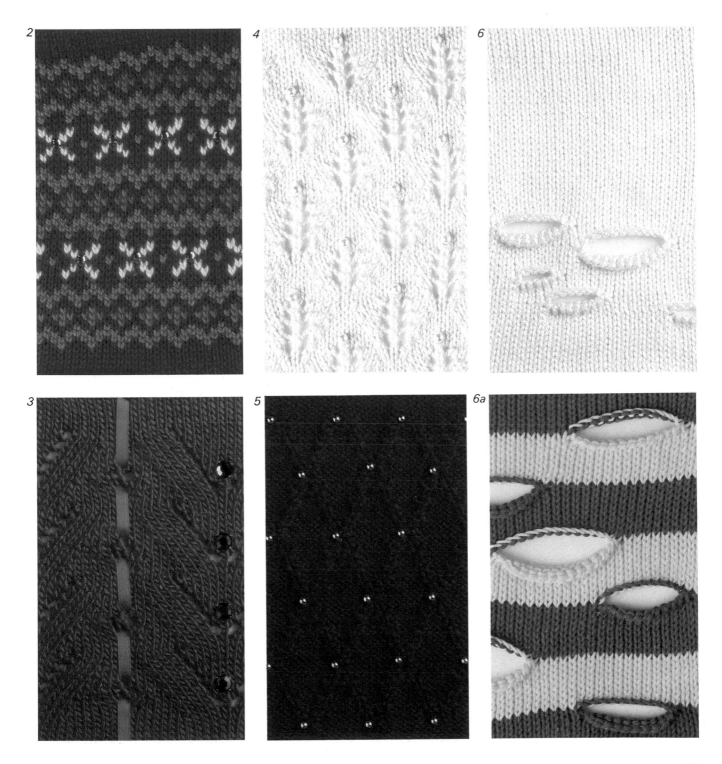

Punchcard for cable and chevron pattern, sample 1.

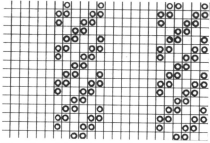

Punchcard for fair isle pattern with diamanté, sample 2.

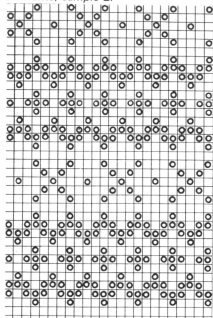

Punchcard for 'fir trees' lace pattern with beads, sample 4.

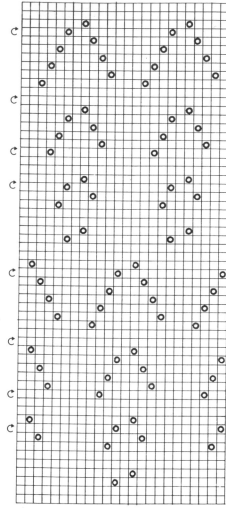

Punchcard for chevron lace pattern with beads or diamanté, sample 3.

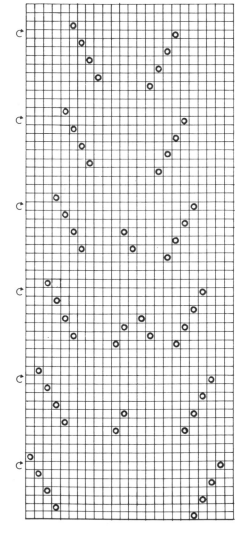

Punchcard for diamond pattern in tuck stitch with beads knitted in, sample 5.

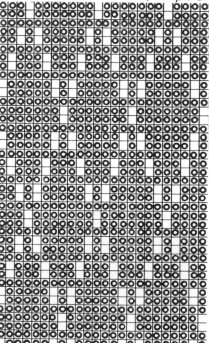

RUCHED KNITTING

BETTY BARNDEN OF TRIFFIC

Betty is particularly interested in the three-dimensional effects of knitting, which began with her famous knitted furniture, using techniques which she is now applying to garments.

Betty won first prize in the Courtelle Hand Knit Award in 1982 and 1984. She makes special garments for exclusive retail sale, and produces hand and machine knit designs for many leading English yarn spinners for promotional and editorial use. Her designs are frequently seen in the national magazines and newspapers.

Betty joined forces with Eddie Pond to form The Triffic Design Company Limited in 1984. They are both graduates of the Royal College of Art: Eddie in Textiles and Betty in Furniture Design, though there are a few years difference in the graduation dates.

Eddie has won many awards for textile design, and has worked with manufacturers all over the world. From 1981 to 1983 he was President of the Society of Industrial Artists and Designers. Triffic is a new venture for Eddie, following the sale of his Paperchase business. With many years experience of design and marketing in textiles, interiors and the gift trade, he sees great potential for a more marketing-oriented business-like approach to creative design in the fashion knitwear industry. He still continues to work as Edward Pond Associates design consultants from the same address as Triffic.

Triffic primarily specialises in the design of creative knitwear, for which Betty has an international reputation, and intends to develop other areas, not only in fashion but in luggage, gifts and interiors.

Betty and her partner Eddie first started working together on contracts from the government's Funded Consultancy Scheme; their biggest success being a range of sweaters manufactured by Ge Ka Knitting, of which the chain of fashion shops called Warehouse sold out in under a week.

The design featured here by Betty Barnden demonstrates her feel for three dimensional knitting. She regards this jacket as more of a craft item than a fashion garment. It has a timelessness which cannot date quickly. Betty believes that interesting stitch and colour work stays looking good and can be worn for several years by teaming it with the appropriate current fashion accessories.

RUCHED JACKET BY BETTY BARNDEN

Photograph on page 44.

MATERIALS: 9 × 50g balls of Wendy Dolce in cream (A), 2 balls in pink (B), 4 × 50g balls of Wendy Pampas in each of 3 colours, blue (C), gold (D) and pink (E).

MEASUREMENTS: To fit 81 to 91cm bust; length 69cm; sleeve seam 48cm.

TENSION: 28 sts and 54 rows to 10cm over pattern.

STITCH PATTERN: (multiple of 24 sts, plus 2) Use punchcard given and work in Fair Isle, with A in feeder 1 throughout. * Place nylon thread over the st at each side of centre, then over every 23rd & 24th st at each side. * With C in feeder 2, K 26 rows. ** Pick up sts marked with nylon thread and put on to corresponding needles. Pull out nylon thread and replace over 12th & 13th sts at each side of centre, then over every 23rd & 24th sts at each side. ** With D in feeder 2, K 26 rows. Pick up sts marked with nylon thread and put on to corresponding needles. Pull out nylon thread. Rep from * to *. With E in feeder 2, K 26 rows. Rep from ** to **. Continue to repeat the last 52 rows, using C, D and E in turn in feeder 2.

BACK (Start at Right Sleeve edge)
Insert punchcard and lock on row 1. Push needles 97 to 48 at left of centre into WP (50 sts). Using B cast on, set TD to MT-2 and K 10 rows. COL. Release punchcard and set machine for Fair Isle. Set TD to MT, RC 000. K 52 rows.

Wrap jacket with rolled tie belt by Betty Barnden. Punchcard design knitted sideways with a ruched effect using different textured yarns for added interest. Neat cuffs and front edges are formed by simply knitting a few extra rows of plain knitting which naturally roll up. Side edge of knitting forms the hem.

Ruched jacket (measurements in cm).

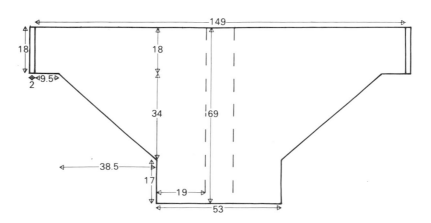

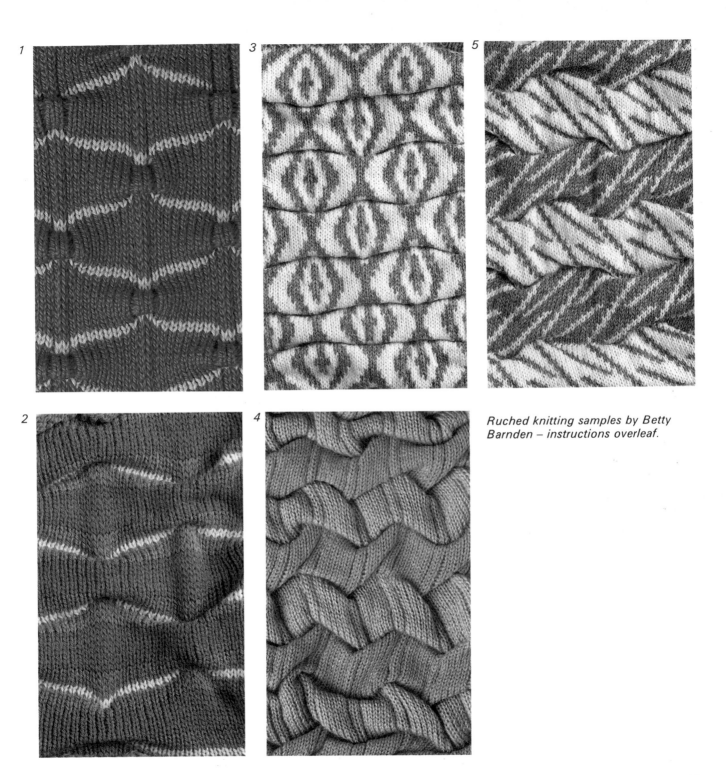

Ruched knitting samples by Betty Barnden – instructions overleaf.

Punchcard for ruched jacket.   *Punchcard A for fair isle sample 3.*   *Punchcard B for mirror effect sample 5.*

Shape Sleeve

[Inc one st at right edge of work on next and foll 11 alt rows, then K 3 rows] 8 times. 146 sts. RC 260. K 1 row. COR.

Shape Side Edge

Cast on 48 sts at beg of next row. 194 sts. K to RC 364. ** Place a marker at each end of last row. K to RC 442. Place a marker at each end of last row. *** K to RC 545.

Shape Left Side and Sleeve

Cast off 48 sts at beg of next row. [K 3 rows, then dec one st at right edge of work on next and foll 11 alt rows] 8 times. 50 sts. K to RC 806. Lock punchcard. Set TD to MT-2. Using B, K 10 rows. Cast off.

LEFT FRONT

Work as for Back to **. Lock punchcard. Set TD to MT-2. Using B, K 10 rows. Cast off.

RIGHT FRONT

Lock punchcard on row 1. Push 194 needles into WP (97 needles at each side of centre). Using B, cast on, set TD to MT-2 and K 10 rows. release punchcard, set TD to MT, RC 442. Work as given for Back from ★★★ to end.

BACK NECK EDGING

Push 40 needles into WP. With wrong side of work facing pick up 40 sts along back neck between markers and place on to needles. Set TD to MT-2. Using B, K 10 rows. Cast off.

BELT

Push 40 needles into WP. Using B, cast on, set TD to MT and K 400 rows. Cast off.

TO MAKE UP

Do not press. Join shoulder seams, sewing ends of back neck edging to edges of front borders. Join side and sleeve seams.

RUCHED KNITTING SAMPLES BY BETTY BARNDEN

Betty Barnden used mainly Wendy yarns for these samples. Photographs on page 45.

1. Two-Colour with Narrow Stripe

This sample uses 2 colours, A and B and requires a multiple of 12 needles, plus 8.
Push needles into WP. Push 2nd needle at each side of centre back into NWP, then every 9th & 12th needle at each side.
Needles are now arranged as follows:

11111111.11.11111111.11.11111111.11.11111111

Using A, cast on and K 2 rows.
★ Using B, K 2 rows, Using A, K 10 rows. ★ Pick up the 2 centre sts on 2nd row in B and put on to corresponding needles, then pick up 24th & 25th, 48th & 49th etc st at each side and put on to corresponding needles. (note these are actual needle numbers, not number of sts) Repeat from ★ to ★. Pick up 12th & 13th, 36th & 37th etc sts at each side of 2nd of last 2 rows in B and put on to corresponding needles. Repeat these 24 rows.

2. Three Colour Sample

This sample uses 3 colours, A, B and C.
Using A, cast on and K 4 rows. Place nylon thread over centre 2 sts, then over every 25th and 26th needle at each side. ★ K 2 rows B, 4 rows A, 8 rows C, 4 rows A. Pick up sts marked with nylon thread on 2nd row in B and put on to corresponding needles. Take out nylon thread. ★ Replace thread over 12th & 13th sts at each side of centre, then every 25th and 26th sts at each side. Rep from ★ to ★. Repeat these 36 rows.

3. Fair Isle Sample

This sample uses 2 colours and Punchcard A. Working in fair isle, K 23 rows. Pick up sts marked X on 2nd row of chart and put on to corresponding needles. K 24 rows. Pick up sts marked Y on 26th row of chart and put on to corresponding needles. K 24 rows. Repeat the last 48 rows.

4. Striped effect

This sample uses 2 colours, A and B and requires a multiple of 10 needles plus 6. The picked up sts are replaced to left or right to give a twisted effect.
Push needles into WP. Push 2nd needle at each side of centre back into NWP, then every 7th and 10th needle at each side. Needles are now arranged as follows:

111111.11.111111.11.111111.11.111111

Using A, K 20 rows. Pick up 2 centre sts from 1st row and replace 10 needles to the right, then pick up 20th & 21st, 40th & 41st etc sts at each side and replace 10 needles to the right. Using B, K 20 rows. Pick up 10th & 11th, 30th & 31st etc sts at each side from 1st row in B and replace 10 needles to the left. Repeat these 40 rows.

5. Mirror Effect

This sample uses 2 colours and Punchcard B. Working in fair isle, K 24 rows. Pick up 2 centre sts from 1st row and 24th & 25th sts at each side and replace 6 needles to the left. K 24 rows. Pick up 12th & 13th sts from 1st row and every 24th & 25th sts at each side and replace 6 needles to the right. Repeat these 48 rows.

Julia Pines' simple top with a slash neck worn with a triangular scarf. The pleated skirt is knitted sideways and attached to a yoke with an elasticated waist.

PLEATING

JULIA PINES

Julia Pines's success as a knitwear designer owes as much to her marketing ability as to her talents as a designer. With a good collection it makes sense to take the financial chance and exhibit at trade fairs world-wide. Julia took this chance and it landed her with orders from large stores in the USA, Milan, Paris, Japan and London. The most expensive venture was naturally the trip to Japan, but fortunately it paid off very well with a three-year contract to Kobe All Style allowing them to produce, market and promote the Julia Pines label under licence in Japan, Hong Kong and Taiwan. They were also to open 13 Julia Pines shops in Hong Kong.

This all came about just four years after gaining her Masters Degree at the Royal College of Art. Before starting her own business Julia gained a lot of valuable experience by acting as a consultant designer to Kay Cosserat as well as spending a season with Dorothee Bis, Paris and Missoni, Milan.

Like most knitwear designers she began designing from her London home but soon decided that business and home life didn't mix. She now has a studio and showroom in Knightsbridge.

Julia studied Fashion Design rather than Textiles at college but concentrated on the use of knitted fabrics and knitwear generally. She has developed a style which she describes as having 'a modern classical feel but with a strong fashion element'. Her new seasons collections, she claims, are intermixable with the old – they are 'on-running'. She enjoys creating interesting jacquard fabrics and seeing the effect colour, and the mixing of colour, can have upon design. Colour changes can break up a simple pattern most interestingly – as it has on the fabric of this top and skirt.

This design shows how the holding position with clever colour changes can produce striking patterns. Here Julia has also demonstrated how one fabric can be used in different ways. By mixing in a finer thread for a couple of rows at regular intervals the fabric can be pleated for a skirt or left loose and 'flat' for a top.

Punchcard for skirt and top.   Repeat for width of card

Repeat for length of card

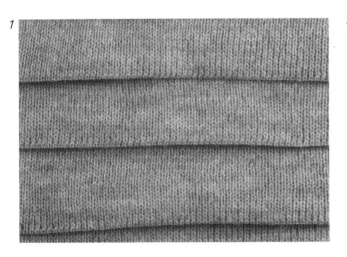

PLEATED SAMPLES BY JULIA PINES

Photographs on page 49.

1. Stocking Stitch Sample in Grey
This uses 2 yarns of different thicknesses – the finer one should be quite thin.
With main yarn, K 30 rows; with fine yarn, K 2 rows; with main yarn K 10 rows; with fine yarn, K 2 rows.
Rep these 44 rows for length required and cast off. Lay knitting on an ironing board and press the pleats in place.

2. Stocking Stitch Sample in Orange
Using a fairly fine yarn, K 12 rows with yarn used double, then K 4 rows with yarn single. Repeat these 16 rows for length required and cast off. Press pleats if necessary.

3. Striped Sample
This needs a machine with ribbing attachment. Cast on for close rib and K 2 rows.
On main bed, counting from the left, transfer 5th and every foll 18th st to the next needle, leave empty needles in NWP. On ribber, counting from the left, transfer 9th and every foll 18th st to the next needle, leave empty needles in NWP. Needles are now arranged as folls:

1111.1111111111111111.1111111111111111.1111111111111

11111111.1111111111111111.1111111111111111.111111111

Knit for the required length and cast off.

4. Box Pleated Sample
This needs a machine with ribbing attachment. Cast on for close rib and K 2 rows.
On main bed, counting from the left, transfer 7th st to the next needle, then every foll 20th and 12th st alternately; leave empty needles in NWP. On ribber, counting from the left, transfer 11th st to next needle, then every foll 11th and 20th st alternately; leave empty needles in NWP. Needles are now arranged as folls:

111111.11111111111111111.1111111111.1111111111111 11111.11111

1111111111.1111111111.1111111111111111111.1111111111 1.111111111

Knit for length required and cast off.
The above samples used Emu yarns.

SKIRT, TOP AND SCARF BY JULIA PINES

MATERIALS: 200g of fine black cotton, such as Twilleys Twenty (M); 9 × 50g balls each of Emu Superwash 4ply in camel (A) and blue (B), 5 balls in black (C). Waist length of elastic.

MEASUREMENTS: To fit 81 to 91cm bust; length of top to neck 62cm; sleeve seam 43cm; length of skirt 78cm.

TENSION: 32 sts and 36 rows to 10cm over stripe patt. TD approx 9 on Knitmaster.

NOTE: When working with 2 colours such as M/A, the first colour (M) goes in feeder 1 and the second colour (A) in feeder 2.

SWEATER (worked in one piece from side to side)
Insert punchcard and lock on row 1. Push 200 needles into WP. Using waste yarn, cast on and K a few rows. COR. Break off waste yarn, release card, set machine for Fair Isle, set TD to MT, RC 000. Using M, K 1 row, then work in pattern as folls:
K 16 rows M/B, 2 rows M only, 16 rows M/A, 2 rows M only. Rep these 36 rows to RC 215.

Shape Armhole
Using M, cast off 90 sts at beg of next row, then cast on 90 sts at end of next row. RC 217.
Cont in pattern to RC 432. Using waste yarn, K a few rows and take off machine.

SLEEVES
Lock card on row 1. Push 140 needles into WP. Using M, cast on, set TD to MT and K 2 rows. Release card, set machine for Fair Isle and starting with M/A, cont in patt to RC 200. Cast off.

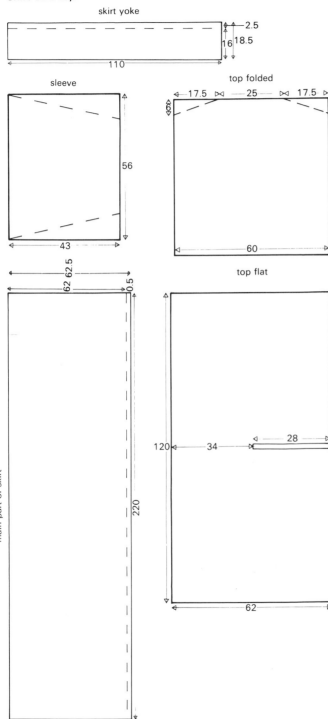

Skirt and top.

skirt yoke

2.5
16 18.5
110

sleeve

56
43

62.5
62
0.5

main part of skirt

220

top folded

17.5 — 25 — 17.5
6
60

top flat

120 — 34 — 28

62

TO MAKE UP

Press work according to instructions on ball band. Join shoulder seams, shaping shoulders as shown by dotted line on diagram. Press seams open. Unravel waste yarn and graft 110 sts for side seam, cast off remaining sts for armhole. Fold sleeves in half and join seam, shaping as shown by dotted line. Press seam open. (Surplus fabric can be machine stitched and cut off if you wish). Sew in sleeves. Turn under hems at lower edge, cuffs and neck and sl st. Press seams.

SKIRT

Yoke

Insert card and lock on row 1. Push 60 needles into WP. Using waste yarn, cast on and K a few rows. Break off waste yarn, set TD to MT, RC 000. Using M, K 1 row. Cont in patt as on Top, but using C instead of B, K to RC 396. Using waste yarn, K a few rows and take off machine.

Main Part

Lock card on row 1. Push 200 needles into WP. Using waste yarn, cast on and K a few rows. Break off waste yarn, release card, set TD to MT, RC 000. Work in patt as folls: 2 rows M only, 16 rows M/C, 2 rows M only, 2 rows M/B, 2 rows M only, 2 rows M/C, 2 rows M only, 2 rows M/A. Rep these 72 rows to RC 792. Using waste yarn, K a few rows and take off machine.

TO MAKE UP

Press work according to instructions on ball band. Pleat main part so that all the stripes in M/A are on top. Sew yoke to skirt, matching stripes. Unravel waste yarn and graft seam. Turn over 2.5cm at top and sl st, threading elastic through. Turn up hem at lower edge and sl st.

SCARF

Insert card and lock on row 1. Push 10 needles at extreme right of bed into WP. Using M, cast on, set TD to MC, RC 000. K 2 rows. Release card and starting with M/B work in patt as on Skirt, inc one st at left on 2nd and every alt row until there are 130 sts – RC 242, then dec one st at left on every alt row until 10 sts rem. At RC 486, cast off. Turn up a hem along straight edge and sl st.

CHAPTER 5

Texture by Mixing Yarns and Detailed Relief Work by Hand

There are endless different textures that can be achieved automatically on the machine by using the punchcard, slipping and tucking procedures. But for something less obviously machine-made looking, and with the interest and appeal of a hand knitted garment, a little hand patterning is worth the extra time it takes. Some of the traditional hand knitting patterns – cables, bobbles and so on – can be done and look especially effective worked in chunky yarns on the heavier gauge machines. See for example the samples knitted on the Bond.

On these pages you'll see some striking and colourful ideas for giving detailed relief to the flat machine-knitted fabric. Here again the holding technique comes into its own.

Interesting texture is also possible with the use of fancy yarns. The choice, of course, is more restricted for machine knitters than hand, unless you have a Bond or chunky machine, but part of the fun of designing your own knitwear is skilfully mixing different textured yarns into a garment. If you are unsure of yourself at first try mixing textures of one or two colours only at a time.

ISABELLA BONNAGE

Isabella specialises in producing the hand-knitted look on a machine. She has three 'chunky' machines and although she has done some designing on the finer gauges, she felt people were prepared to pay more for the home-made look.

Isabella studied at the Central School of Art, a course that concentrated more on furnishings than fashions. So her future involvement in knitting was a new area of textile design for Isabella.

On gaining her BA, Isabella's first job was as manageress of a small London boutique. Here she realised the opportunities for making a going concern of knitting. She noticed the saleability of hand knits and just how much people were prepared to pay for anything hand made. With most other areas of textile design, to start out on one's own usually requires a substantial amount of financial investment for space and equipment, rewarded by relatively slow returns – especially if only one in three designs actually sell. But Isabella discovered that with machine knitting, all that is required is a machine plus a modest sum up front for yarns and outworkers.

Isabella launched into her business, with a little help from her bank manager, selling chunky knits from a studio in King's Cross, London. She immediately aimed at the hand-knit market using the machine as a means to a quicker end. Having always felt 'sickened' at the exploitation of hand-knitters, she felt a little happier because although she paid her knitters the going hand-knitting rates, she knew they'd be able to complete the garments in a fraction of the time on their machines. She found that every design brought in money, for even the 'mistakes' were saleable. She and a friend hired a little boutique in San Tropez for the summer months selling Isabella Bonnage knits with her friend's leather fashions. They returned in time to show at the autumn/winter collections in London. Henceforth Isabella's orders grew for boutiques in England and abroad.

Isabella tries to exploit the chunky machine to its

Isabella Bonnage's 'Sloppy Joe' cowl neck sweater with three-quarter length sleeves. The textured effect is achieved by the use of yarns and stitchwork.

fullest, experimenting with interesting yarns and textures. This of course, is one of the main advantages these machines have over the finer gauge machines. The chunky will knit almost anything, although yarns thinner than 4 ply need to be knitted double or triple. Knitting is quick, and mistakes such as dropped stitches are easier to pick up and correct. However, a great deal more hand work is required for many patterns.

Isabella finds it is the yarn itself that first inspires the design. She concentrates first on finding a suitable 'fabric' by means of stitch samples, then thinks about the design. She rarely puts pen to paper but works her ideas directly onto the machine. Sometimes she works out the measurements from an old sweater, but years of experience have now saved her the trouble of completing a sample garment before commissioning her knitters. She now knows which neck suits which body, and can work out their instructions from just the stitch sample.

The sweater featured in this book by Isabella is one example of how the chunky machine can compete with hand knitting. It combines a fluffy yarn with a bouclé in an interesting honeycomb effect achieved by picking up stitches at regular intervals from the row 11 rows below and knitting them into the 12th row.

HONEYCOMB STITCH SWEATER BY ISABELLA BONNAGE

For chunky machines.

MATERIALS: 9 × 25g balls of Copley Sundae (M), 4 × 25g balls of Copley Sandpiper in each of 2 contrast colours, Pink (A) & Beige (B).

MEASUREMENTS: To fit 86 to 97cm bust; length to neck 71cm; sleeve seam 38cm.

TENSION: 11 sts and 24 rows to 10cm over pattern.

BACK and FRONT (alike)
Push 67 needles into WP. Set TD to MT (or insert appropriate Keyplate for Bond machine). Using waste yarn cast on and K a few rows. Break off waste yarn and work in patt as folls: Using A, K 2 rows. Using M, K 9 rows. Pick up loop of 4th and every foll 6th st on first row of A and put on to corresponding needles. K 1 row. Using B, K 2 rows. Using M, K 9 rows. Pick up loop of 7th and every foll 6th st on first row of B and put on to corresponding needles. K 1 row. These 24 rows form patt and are rep throughout. Cont until 110 rows in all have been worked, thus ending with a 2nd row in B.

Shape Armholes
** Keeping pattern correct, [dec one st at each end of next and foll 4 alt rows, then work 3 rows] twice. Work the next 10 rows in A instead of M, at the same time dec one st at each end of next and every alt row. Work 2 rows in B. Work 10 rows in M, dec one st at each end of next and every alt row. Pick up sts for pattern and K 1 row. ** Cast off rem 27 sts.

Hem
Push 45 needles into WP. With wrong side of work facing put sts of first row on to needles as folls: one st on first needle, [2 sts on next needle, one st on next needle] to end. Unravel waste yarn. Using M, K 22 rows. Cast off loosely.

SLEEVES
Push 61 needles into WP. Work as given for Back,

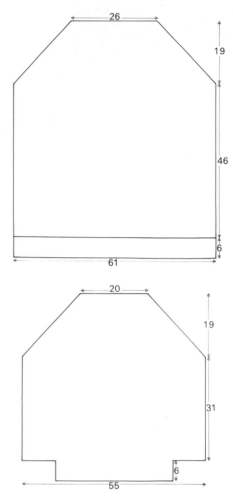

but starting patt with B instead of A, cont until 74 rows have been worked, thus ending with a 2nd row in B.

Shape Top
Work as given for Back from ** to **. Cast off rem 21 sts.

Cuff
Push 30 needles into WP. With wrong side facing put sts of first row on to needles, 3 sts on first needle, then 2 sts on every needle to end. Unravel waste yarn. Using M, K 28 rows. Cast off loosely.

Punchcard for honeycomb sweater.

COLLAR

Push 90 needles into WP. Using M, cast on and K 12 rows. Pick up loops from first row and put on to needles to make a hem, then K a further 70 rows, Cast off loosely.

TO MAKE UP

Do not press. Join raglan seams. Join side and sleeve seams. Turn up hems at lower edge and cuffs and sl st. Join seam of Collar, then sew cast off edge of Collar to neck edge, with seam at centre back.

TEXTURE SAMPLES BY ISABELLA BONNAGE

Photographs on page 56.

1. Honeycomb Pattern

This stitch is best worked in two contrasting types of yarn. We have used a Mohair (M) and a Cotton yarn (C).

It requires a number of sts divisible by 6 plus 1.

Using M, cast on and K 4 rows.

* Using C, K 2 rows; using M, K 7 rows. Pick up loop from 4th and every foll 6th st on first row in C and put on to corresponding needles, K 1 row.

Using C, K 2 rows; using M, K 7 rows. Pick up loop from 7th and every foll 6th st on first of last 2 rows in C and put on to corresponding needles. K 1 row.

Repeat from *.

2. Striped Sample

This sample is worked in st st and shows the effect which can be obtained by using different types of yarn – we have used a suede type yarn and a nobbly cotton, working in stripes of 2 rows suede, 1 row cotton throughout.

3. Lacy Pattern

This sample requires an odd number of stitches. Cast on and K 2 rows.

Counting from the left, put 2nd and every alt st on to next needle to the right, leaving the empty needles in WP. K 2 rows.

Counting from the left, put 3rd and every alt st on to next needle to the right, leaving the empty needles in WP. K 2 rows.

Rep these 4 rows.

4. Weaving

This is a sample of weaving worked with a smooth yarn for the knitting and a mohair yarn for the weaving.

Insert the punchcard and work weaving as given in your instruction book.

All the samples above used Copley yarns.

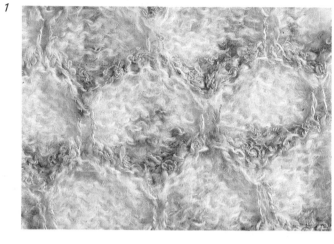

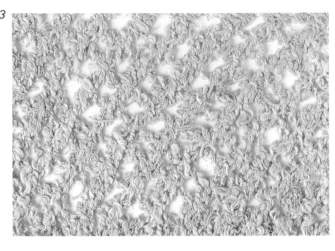

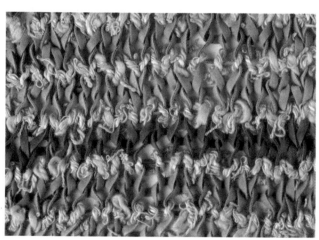

SWEATER WITH CHECKED RIDGES AND COLOURED 'BLOBS' BY JUDY DODSON

MATERIALS: For all sizes 3 × 250g cones of Rowan Mercerised Cotton in Natural (M), 1 cone in Silver (A), small amounts in Pink (B), Blue (C), Green (D) and Yellow (E).

MEASUREMENTS: To fit 81 (86, 91, 97)cm bust; length to shoulders 62cm; sleeve seam 50cm.

TENSION: 32 sts and 44 rows to 10cm over st-st, TD approx 7. RT is approx TD-2.

BACK

Push 135 (143, 151, 159) needles into WP for 1/1 rib. Using M, cast on, set TD to RT and K 40 rows. Transfer sts to main bed, inc one st at end of row. 136 (144, 152, 160) sts. Insert punchcard and lock on row 1. Set TD to MT, RC 000. K 30 rows. * Release punchcard. Place A in feeder 2, K 1 row. Disconnect RC and K 5 rows. Pick up loops from first row of checks and place on needles to make a tuck. Lock punchcard. Take M and A out of yarn feeders. * Push 32 (36, 40, 44) needles at right and 92 (96, 100, 104) needles at left into HP, leaving 12 needles in WP. With D, + + set machine for

A slash neck is cleverly incorporated into the detailing of this design. Note how the 'ridges' running across the shoulders divide for the neck opening.

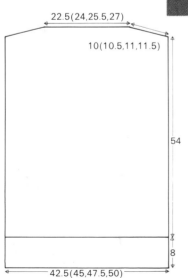

22.5(24,25.5,27)

10(10.5,11,11.5)

54

8

42.5(45,47.5,50)

Sweater with checked ridges and coloured 'blobs'.

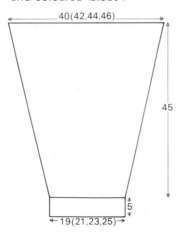

40(42,44,46)

45

5

19(21,23,25)

Punchcard for sweater with checked 'blobs'.

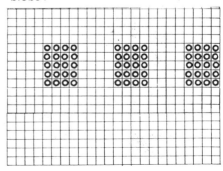

Repeat for length of card.

partial knitting and K 1 row. [Push one needle at each end into HP, K 1 row] 5 times. (2 needles left in WP). Still working on the same 12 sts, [push 2 needles at opposite end to carriage into WP, K 1 row] 4 times. [Push one needle at opposite end to carriage into WP, K 1 row] twice. + + Break off D. ** Push all needles back into WP, unlock punchcard. With A in feeder 1 and M in feeder 2, K 5 rows. Reset RC and K 1 row. Pick up loops from first of the last 6 rows and place on to needles to make a tuck. Break off A, lock punchcard and replace M in feeder 1. ** RC 32. K 32 rows, then rep from * to *. Push 51 (55, 59, 63) needles at right and 73 (77, 81, 85) needles at left into HP. Using C, rep from + + to + +. Break off C. Push these needles into HP. Leaving 108 (112, 116, 120) needles at right and 16 (20, 24, 28) needles at left in HP, push rem 12 needles into WP. Using B, rep from + + to + +. Break off B and rep from ** to **. RC 66. K 48 rows, then rep from * to *. Push 72 (76, 80, 84) needles at right and 40 (44, 48, 52) needles at left into HP, leaving 24 needles in WP. with E, + + + set machine for partial knitting and K 1 row. [Push 3 needles at opposite end to carriage and one needle at carriage end into HP, K 1 row] 5 times, push one needle at each end into HP, K 1 row (leaving 2 needles in WP). Push one needle at each end back into WP, K 1 row. [Push 4 needles at opposite end to carriage into WP, K 1 row] 5 times. + + + Break off E and rep from ** to **. RC 116. K 26 rows, then rep from * to *. Push 36 (40, 44, 48) needles at right and 88 (92, 96, 100) needles at left into HP. Using B, rep from + + to + +. Break off B and rep from ** to **. RC 144. K 36 rows, then rep from * to *. Push 18 (22, 26, 30) needles at right and 106 (110, 114, 118) needles at left into HP. Using E, rep from + + to + +. Break off E and push these needles into HP. Leaving 106 (110, 114, 118) needles at right and 18 (22, 26, 30) needles in HP, push rem 12 needles into WP. Using D, rep from + + to + +. Break off D and repeat from ** to **. RC 182. K 26 rows, then rep from * to *. Push 76 (80, 84, 88) needles at right and 36 (40, 44, 48) needles at left into HP. Using C, rep from + + + to + + +. Break off C and rep from ** to **. RC 210. K 30 rows. RC 240.

Shape Shoulders

[Push 10 (11, 12, 13) needles at opposite end to carriage into HP, K 1 row] 4 times. [Push 11 needles at opposite end to carriage into HP, K 1 row] twice. [Push all needles at opposite end to carriage back into WP, K 1 row] twice. Unlock punchcard, place A in feeder 2 and K 6 rows. Pick up loops from first of these 6 rows and place on machine to make a tuck. Slip 31 (33, 35, 37) sts at each end on to waste yarn and take off machine. Using M, K 1 row, then cast off remaining 74 (78, 82, 86) sts.

FRONT

Work as given for Back, but reverse colours on the last 6 rows at shoulder by placing A in feeder 1 and M in feeder 2. With right side of work facing place 31 (33, 35, 37) sts of one shoulder on to machine, then with wrong side facing place the corresponding sts of back shoulder on to the same needles. Unravel waste yarn and cast sts off tog. Repeat for the other shoulder.

SLEEVES

Push 59 (63, 67, 71) needles into WP for 1/1 rib. Using M, cast on, set TD to RT and K 24 rows. Transfer sts to main bed, inc 3 (5, 7, 9) sts evenly across the row. 62 (68, 74, 80) sts. Insert punchcard and lock on row 1. Set TD to MT, RC 000. K 26 rows, inc one st at each end of every 5th row. 72 (78, 84, 90) sts. Continue to inc at each end of every 5th row until there are 120 (126, 132, 138) sts, then at each end of every 10th row until there are 128 (134, 140, 146) sts, AT THE SAME TIME work in patt as folls: Rep from * to *. Push 30 (33, 36, 39) needles at each end into HP. With E, rep from + + to + +. Break off E and rep from ** to **. RC 28. K 32 rows, then rep from * to *. Push 23 (26, 28, 32) needles at right and 51 (54, 57, 60) needles at left into HP. With D, rep from + + to + +. Break off D and push these needles into HP. Leaving 56 (59, 62, 65) needles at right and 18 (21, 24, 27) needles at left in HP, push rem 12 needles into WP. With C, rep from + + to + +. Break off C and rep from ** to **. RC 62. K 44 rows, then rep from * to *. Push 52 (55, 58, 61) needles at right and 28 (31, 34, 37) needles at left into HP. With B, rep from + + + to + + +. Break off B and rep from ** to **. RC 108. K 28 rows, then rep from * to *. Push 38 (41, 44, 47) needles at right and 66 (69, 72, 75) needles at left into HP. With C, rep from + + to + +. Break off C and rep from ** to **. RC 138. K 34 rows, then rep from * to *. Push 32 (35, 38, 41) needles at right and 80 (83, 86, 89) needles at left into HP. With E, rep from + + to + +. Break off E and push these needles into HP. Leaving 70 (73, 76, 79) needles at right and 42 (45, 48, 51) needles at left in HP, push rem 12 needles into WP. With D, rep from + + to + +. Break off D and rep from ** to **. RC 174. K 26 rows. RC 200. Cast off loosely.

TO MAKE UP

Press work according to instructions on cone. Sew in sleeves, placing centre of sleeves to shoulder seams. Join side and sleeve seams. Press seams.

CORDING AND HOLDING SAMPLES BY JUDY DODSON

Photographs on page 60.

1. Zig-Zags with Cording

This sample has been worked over 50 sts, using 4 colours, A, B, C and D. Using A, K 2 rows. [Push 5 needles at right into HP, K 2 rows] twice. Push 5 needles at right into HP. (35 needles now in WP). * Using B, K 4 rows on these sts, pick up loops from first of these 4 rows and put on to needles. * Using C, [push 5 needles at right into HP, K 2 rows] 3 times, then push 5 more needles into HP (15 needles now in WP). Rep from * to *. Using D, [push 5 needles to right into HP, K 2 rows] twice. Push all needles back into WP. Rep from * to *. Using C, K 1 row. COR. [push 5 needles at left into HP, K 2 rows] twice. Rep from * to *. Using D, [push 5 needles at left into HP, K 2 rows] 5 times. Rep from * to *. Using A, [push 5 needles at left into HP, K 2 rows] twice. Push all needles back into WP and rep from * to *. Cont in this way, varying length and width of zig-zags as required.

2. Horizontal Cords

Where a cord is required, push all needles into HP except the ones needed for the cord. Using contrast colour, K 4 or 6 rows on these sts, then pick up loops from first of these rows and put on to needles. Push all needles back into WP.

3. Gathered Checks and Cords

This sample has been worked in 2 pieces, with 22 sts in each, using 3 colours, A, B and C.
For 1st piece, using A, K 32 rows. Using B, K 6 rows, pick up loops from first of these rows and put on to needles. Using C, K 64 rows. Cast off.
For 2nd piece, using C, K 64 rows. Using B, work cord as 1st piece. Using A, K 32 rows. Cast off.
Push 40 needles into WP. With wrong side of 1st piece facing pick up 20 sts along side of each colour and place on to needles. With B, K 6 rows, pick up loops from first of these rows and put on to needles. Using waste yarn, K a few rows and take off machine. With right side facing, replace sts on same needles, unravelling waste yarn, then with wrong side of 2nd piece facing, pick up 20 sts along side of each colour and place on to needles (alternating the colours as in picture) and cast off all sts together.

4. Cording and Holding

This sample has been worked over 68 sts, using 3 colours, A, B and C. With A, K 6 rows. ** Leave 4 needles in WP, [push next 3 needles into HP, leave next 16 sts in WP] 3 times, push next 3 needles into HP, leave rem 4 needles in WP. Using B, K 10 rows, dropping off the loops over needles in HP after every 4th row. Push all needles back into WP, K [2 rows C, 2 rows A] twice, 2 rows C. Over the centre 10 sts of each group of 16, pick up loops from the 1st row in C and place them on to corresponding needles. Repeat from ** but reversing stripes in A and C on next and every alt repeat. Reverse illustrated to show structure.

5. Cording and Holding with Twisted Loops

This sample has been worked over 72 sts, using 4 colours, A, B, C and D. Using A, K 4 rows. ** Leave first 4 needles in WP, [push 16 needles into HP, leave next 8 needles in WP] twice, push 16

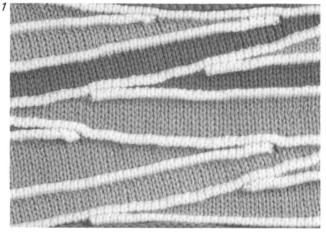

1

2

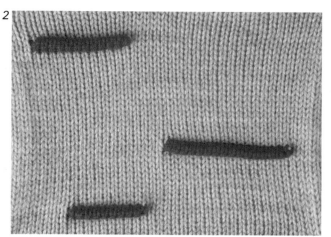

3

4

5

needles into HP, leave rem 4 needles in WP. Using B, K 6 rows, dropping off the loops over the needles in HP after every 3rd row. ** Push all needles back into WP. Using A, K 2 rows. Repeat from ** to ** but using C instead of B. Working on one set of loops, take the top 6 strands and bring them towards you and under the bottom 6 strands, continue twisting until they form a tight twist. Using the double transfer tool, pick up the centre 2 sts on first of the 2 rows in A behind the twist, bring them in front of the twist and replace on to needles, catching in one thread of the twist. Work across all loops in this way. Using A, K 6 rows, then make a tuck by picking up the loops of first of these 6 rows over the 8 sts in C only and placing them on to

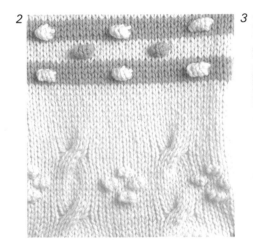

needles. Repeat from ⋆⋆, using D instead of B and B instead of C, then rep from ⋆⋆ again, using C instead of B and D instead of C.
Repeat these 60 rows.

BOND MACHINE SAMPLES

The samples were all worked on a Bond using chunky yarns but most of these could also be worked on any machine using finer yarn.

1. Ladder Stitch

Cast on and K 10 rows. Counting from the left, drop the 10th st from needle and run it down 5 rows. Pick up the st, leaving the loose strands behind it and put the st back on the needle. Repeat with every 10th st along the row.
K 10 rows. Counting from the left, drop 5th and every following 10th st and make a ladder as before. Repeat these 20 rows.

2. Bobbles

Using a separate length of main or contrast yarn, K2 or 3 sts by hand at chosen position, from left to right, then K the same sts again by hand from right to left. K1 or 3 more rows in this way, then pick up the original 2 or 3 sts on the row before the bobble and put the loops on to the needles (thus leaving the bobble behind the work). Repeat as required. Tie the ends of yarn firmly behind each bobble. The bobbles can be worked in stripes, as on the sample, or clustered and mixed with cables.

3. Garter Stitch Ridges

To work a line of garter stitch across the work, start at one side, take the latchet tool and place into the loop below first st, drop the st off the needle – it will now run down 1 row. Hook it up with the latchet tool as if working rib and replace it on the needle. Repeat with every st along the row. K 2 rows. Repeat as required.

To work blocks as on sample, or diamonds, work in the same way, dropping only the stitches where you want the patterns to come.

4. Loop Stitches

With a spare length of yarn make 2 loops about 2 to 3 cm long. Push out needles 2 and 98 and hang the loops on to them.

Take out 1 rod from the double weighted hem, hang the rod between the loops and push against the knitting.

Take the yarn out of the carriage, or use a contrast yarn and keeping it in your hand, K the sts along the row one by one, passing the yarn over and under the rod – i.e. K one st, (pass yarn over, K the next st, pass yarn under, K the next st) all along the row. K one row to 'fix' the sts. Take out the rod and pull knitting down carefully. You can work this right along the row, or mix it with some sts knitted in between – as shown in the sample.

SWEATER WITH TUCKS BY LOUISE PARSONS

Photograph on page 64.

MATERIALS: 10 × 50g balls of Pingouin Fil d'Ecosse no 5 in main colour (M), oddments in 2 or more contrast colours as reqd.

MEASUREMENTS: To fit 86 to 91cm bust; length 57cm; sleeve seam 45cm.

TENSION: 28 sts and 40 rows to 10cm over st st. Rib tension is approx MT-3.

NOTE: To work a tuck, put all needles into HP except the ones being used for the tuck. Using main colour or contrast as reqd, K 6 rows on these needles, then pick up the loops from the first of these 6 rows and put on to the needles.

BACK

Push 149 needles into WP for 1/1 rib. Using M, cast on, set TD to RT and K 40 rows. Transfer sts to main bed. Counting from the left, transfer 25th and every foll 25th st on to the next needle, leaving the empty needles in NWP to form vertical lines. You now have 6 panels of 24 sts with one needle in NWP between each. 144 sts. Set TD to MT. RC 000. K 30 rows. Disconnect RC. Counting from the left, work a tuck on 2nd panel of 24 sts, push needles into HP. Work on tuck on 4th and 6th panels of 24 sts. Push all needles back into WP. Reconnect RC. K 30 rows. Disconnect RC. Counting from the left, work a tuck on 1st, 3rd and 5th panels of 24 sts. Push all needles back into WP. Reconnect RC. Rep these 60 rows twice more, working tucks in M or contrast colour at random as reqd, then K to RC 196.

Shape Shoulders

Cast off 38 sts at beg of next 2 rows. Using waste yarn, K a few rows on rem 68 sts and take off machine.

FRONT

Work as given for Back to RC 186.

Shape Neck

Push 91 needles at opposite end to carriage into HP and cont on rem 53 sts. K 1 row. Cast off 3 sts at beg of next and foll 4 alt rows. RC 196. Cast off. Push centre 38 needles back into WP; using waste yarn, K a few rows and take off machine. Push rem 53 needles back into WP and work to match first side, reversing shaping.

SLEEVES

Push 59 needles into WP for 1/1 rib. Using M, cast on, set TD to RT and K 40 rows. Transfer sts to main bed. Counting from the left, transfer 5th and every foll 25th st on to the next needle, leaving the empty needles in NWP. 56 sts. Set TD to MT, RC 000. K 30 rows, inc one st at each end of every 3rd row. 76 sts. Disconnect RC. Counting from the left, make a tuck on first panel of 24 sts, then over panel of 14 sts at right. Push all needles back into WP. Reconnect RC. Continue in pattern as set, working tucks after every 30 rows on alternate panels as on back, AT THE SAME TIME inc one st at each end of every 3rd row, working the extra sts into patt, until there are 144 sts, then K to RC 150. Cast off loosely.

NECKBAND
Push 143 needles into WP for 1/1 rib. Using M, cast on, set TD to RT and K 14 rows. Transfer sts to main bed.
Join left shoulder seam. With wrong side of work facing pick up 143 sts round neck edge, including sts on waste yarn and put on to needles. Using M, cast sts off tog loosely.

TO MAKE UP
Press work lightly according to instructions on ball band. Join right shoulder seam and neckband. Sew in sleeves, placing centre of sleeves to shoulder seams. Join side and sleeve seams. Press seams.

SWEATER WITH MULTI-COLOURED TUCKS BY JONES/BROTHER

By courtesy of Brother Fashion magazine. Photograph on page 64.

MATERIALS: 6 (6, 6, 7, 7) 50g balls of Pingouin Laine Nylon in black (M), 1 × 50g ball each of Pingouin Perle No 5 in red (A), blue (B), green (C) and yellow (D).

MEASUREMENTS: To fit 81 (86, 91, 97, 102)cm bust; length 37cm; sleeve seam 36cm.

TENSION: 30 sts and 35 rows to 10cm over st st. 28 sts and 86 rows to 10cm over pattern for front. (TD approx 8 on Jones machines)

NOTE: When working with 2 colours, such as M/A, the first colour (M) goes in feeder 1 and the second colour (A) in feeder 2. Where only one colour is given, this goes in feeder 1.

Sweater with tucks (measurements in cm).

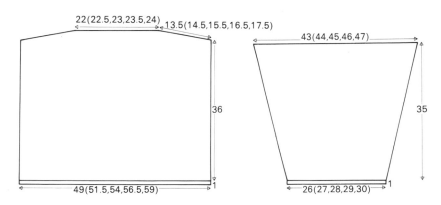

Two designs depicting ridges of relief patterning by tucking.
Left: 'Cropped' multi-coloured sweater courtesy of Brother Fashion Magazine*.
Right: Vertical brick pattern with occasional dashes of contrasting colour, by knitwear designer Louise Parsons.

*Jones + Brother produce their own knitting publication, Brother Fashion, released twice a year in April and October. The magazine, edited by Susan Nutbeam, aims to keep machine knitters informed of the latest fashion colours, yarns and knitting techniques. Available from Jones + Brother dealers, Woolco, A&N Stores, Rackhams and John Lewis. Subscriptions directly from: Jones + Brother, Shepley St., Guide Bridge, Audenshaw, Manchester M34 5JD.

FRONT

Insert card A and lock on row 1. Push 138 (146, 154, 162, 170) needles into WP. * Using waste yarn, cast on and K a few rows. COL. Break off waste yarn, join in D. Set TD to 3, K 6 rows; TD 6, K 1 row; TD 5, K 6 rows. Pick up sts from first row in D and put them on to needles to form a hem, unravel waste yarn. COR. Set TD to 8, RC 000. Join in M and K 3 rows. Release card, set machine for Fair Isle and K 1 row. * K 4 rows M/B, 2 rows M, [depress both part buttons, K 6 rows A, pick up loops from first of these 6 rows and put on to needles to form tucks, release part buttons, K 2 rows M] 4 times. These 38 rows form the rep of patt; cont in patt, working Fair Isle rows alternately in C, A, D, C, B, D, and A, work working tucks as follows: 2 in D, 2 in B, 4 in C, 2 in B, 2 in A, 4 in D, 2 in A, 2 in C, 4 in B, 2 in C, 2 in D. Continue to RC 308, thus ending with 2 rows in M.

Shape Shoulders

Using M/B, cast off 18 (19, 21, 22, 24) sts at beg of next 2 rows, then 18 (20, 21, 23, 24) sts at beg of next 2 rows. 66 (68, 70, 72, 74) sts rem.

Neckband

Set TD to 5. Using A, K 6 rows; TD 6, K 1 row; TD 3, K 6 rows. Pick up loops from first row in A and put on to needles. Cast off loosely.

BACK

Insert card B and lock on row 1. Push 148 (156, 164, 172, 180) needles into WP. Using B instead of D, work as for Back from * to *. Cont in patt, working Fair Isle rows in A, D, C, B in turn. Work to RC 132.

Shape Shoulders

Using M/A, cast off 20(22, 23, 25, 26) sts at beg of next 2 rows, then 21 (22, 24, 25, 27) sts at beg of next 2 rows. 66 (68, 70, 72, 74) sts rem.

Neckband

Using E, work as given for Front.

LEFT SLEEVE

Insert card B and lock on row 1. Push 80 (82, 86, 88, 92) needles into WP. Using C instead of D, work as given for Front from * to *. Cont in patt, working Fair Isle rows in B, A, D, C in turn, at the same time inc one st at each end of every 4th row until there are 130 (132, 136, 138, 142) sts, then cont without shaping to RC 124. Cast off loosely.

RIGHT SLEEVE

Work as given for Left Sleeve, but working hem in A and working Fair Isle in D, C, B, A in turn.

TO MAKE UP

Press work according to instructions on ball band. Join shoulder seams and ends of neckband. Sew in sleeves, placing centre of sleeves to shoulder seams. Join side and sleeve seams. Press seams.

Sweater with multi-coloured tucks (measurements in cm).

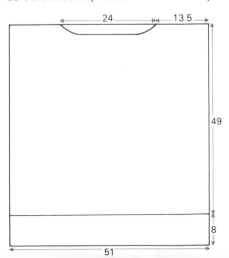

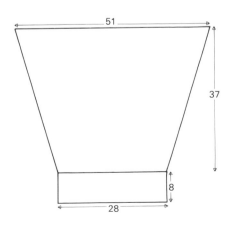

Punchcards for sweater with multi-coloured tucks.

Card A   Card B

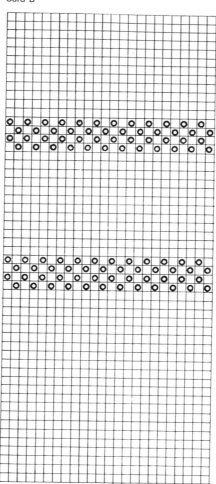

Shaping

Now that you are (hopefully) inspired into creating your own exciting fabrics and have perhaps decided on one or more that you'd like to knit up into a garment, the next stage is working out the shape. Until you have become fairly proficient at designing workable shapes and accurately translating the tension of your swatch into stitches and rows, it is advisable to stick to simple (and currently very fashionable) shapes, especially if also having to calculate punchcard pattern repeats and so on.

In this section of the book Knitmaster Design Studio explain in the chapter about charting devices how to take measurements and draw up a basic pattern block, and adapt it accordingly. Also explained in this chapter with the help of a chart, is how to calculate your rows and needles if you do not have a gauge, computer or charting device to do it for you, plus the use of graphs. And last, but not least, how to estimate the amount of yarn to buy before you start knitting.

Chapter 7 explains another interesting area of design open to machine knitters – cut and sew.

The fabric for the bold checked jacket was knitted on a Jones Chunky machine by the intarsia patterning technique, and made up from a Vogue Individualist pattern – an American Designer Original. Its straight and loose shape is ideal for cut and sew. Vilene was used on the fronts, back shoulders, pockets and sleeve edges. The top and skirt are from another Vogue pattern, the top having a high tucked collar and peplum waist interfaced with Vilene. The semi-circular skirt was knitted on a standard Jones machine using the holding technique for the shaping in preference to cut and sew. Pattern on page 81.

A luxurious evening-look angora sweater with asymmetrical patterning. Designed by the Knitmaster Design Studio*. Pattern on page 75.

*Knitmaster are the only knitting machine company to have a design studio. The Knitmaster Design Studio, who have supplied this design and the 'Cobweb' dress (page 33) and have written the chapters on electronic machines and charting devices, is staffed by highly qualified designers and fully trained technicians. Together as a team they research fashion trends, test new machinery and equipment and are in the forefront of garment and textile design and development.

They also produce garments and patterns for their own publication, *Modern Knitting*, as well as for specialist and women's interest magazines.

CHAPTER 6

Measurements, Patterns and Charting Devices

CHARTING DEVICES

Many machines can be fitted with a charting device. This is where special sheets or rolls of plastic or paper, with the diagram outline of the pattern printed or drawn on, are fed into a device which indicates, as you knit, row by row where to increase or decrease.

You will be supplied with some standard patterns but you can (and will surely want to) draw your own pattern shapes on to them. You could, if you liked, even trace off commercial dress patterns.

These devices are called different names according to the make of the machine. (I've called mine a few names too but they're not printable!)

In this chapter The Knitmaster Design Studio explain how to design your own patterns and use them on a charting device. The Knitmaster system is called Knitradar but the basic instructions are the same for all the systems.

In 1972 Knitmaster introduced a revolutionary new system of following a machine knitting pattern. The completely new system not only made it simple to follow a knitting pattern, but also made the pattern flexible – allowing any yarn and stitch pattern to be used, and minor alterations to be made to the shape quite easily. The piece of equipment that made all this possible was Knitmaster's Knitradar and it proved so popular that other machine manufacturer's quickly followed on with their own versions of it.

To avoid confusion this chapter is written for Knitmaster's Knitradar. Those of you who own different makes of this device will know that only Knitmaster's Knitradar is 1/2 scale whereas all other makes are 1/1 scale. This will make no difference to the instructions given except that you will need a larger working surface and larger sheets of paper.

In this chapter you are going to learn how to make your own knitradar patterns – an important step in designing for yourself.

EQUIPMENT YOU WILL NEED

To make a Knitradar pattern you will find it useful to have the following pieces of equipment: a Triangular Half Scale, a Freeline Drawer, a Knitradar Tracing Roll and some large sheets of paper. The Triangular Half Scale will automatically convert full scale measurements to half scale measurements, so we don't have to consider the 1/2 scale of knitradar at all in the following instructions.

TAKING YOUR MEASUREMENTS

The basic measurements should be taken in centimetres but if you use a tape measure that shows inches too you will be able to see what the equivalent in inches is at a glance. Many people feel happier if they can refer back to inches as a check.

The measurements for a average size 12 have been inserted to give you a guideline, and the order they are in will help when it comes to drawing the pattern.

1. Across chest	34cm	This measurement is taken above the bust, between the armpits.
2. Back neck	14cm	This is virtually impossible to measure from the body because knitting tends to stretch at the neckline giving a false finished measurement. 14cm is the smallest measurement you will be able to get over your head, and will give a neat neckline. Please note that men's heads tend to be a little larger while children's are not much smaller.
3. Front neck depth	7cm	The same is true for this measurement as the back neck measurement.
4. Shoulder drop	3cm	This measurement allows for the slope of shoulders and, again is one that you will not be able to measure from the body. However, 3cm is the average for all adult sizes and 2cm for children's sizes.
5. Armhole depth	18cm	Take this measurement from the bone where your arm joins your shoulder and measure in a straight line down to where you want the armhole to finish. 18cm is really the minimum armhole depth for a size 12.
6. Bust	86cm	
7. Back neck to waist	42cm.	
8. Waist	66cm	
9. Hips	92cm	
10. Waist to hips	12cm	When making a knitting pattern, we don't measure down from the waist to the largest part of the hips, but from the waist down to the hipbone.
11. Sleeve length	56cm	Measure from the bone where the arm joins the shoulder down to the top of your hand. This measurement is taken with the arm straight.
12. Wrist	20cm	This is not the actual wrist measurement, but the smallest measurement that will go over a woman's hand. Measure round the widest part of the hand with the thumb tucked in as a guideline.

DRAWING A BASIC PATTERN

The basic pattern is, in fact, the pattern for a classic crew-neck sweater. It has the normal amount of ease added and will be a neat, comfortable fit. It will be used as starting point for most of your patterns.

Using a large sheet of paper, construct your pattern by following, in sequence, the numbers on the diagrams and referring to the corresponding note. Remember to use your Triangular Half Scale or your pattern will be full scale instead of half scale.

1. Shoulder width is the same as the across chest measurement. This is for ease of knitting and also because the stitches tend to spread at the shoulders.

2. Drop the back neck 2cm and curve the line up to the shoulder as shown in the diagram. Drop the front neck 7cm and curve up to the shoulder. When adding the neckband, care should be taken not to lose the stretch in the knitting or this small neckline will not go over your head. If in doubt make a wider neckline.

3. Drop shoulder line 3cm. Line number (1) can be rubbed out now since it does not form part of your pattern.

4. Draw in armhole depth.

5. 5cm ease should be added to the complete bust measurement. Remember to halve 'all-round' measurements because you're only drawing half the pattern. Curve the armhole as shown in the

diagram. The Freeline Drawer will help you to draw curves.

6. Although you won't need the waistline for sweaters, it's a good guideline and will be needed for dresses.

7. The same is true for the hipline.

8. Draw in the top arm measurement.

9. Draw, on one side of the centre, a diagonal line which is the same measurement as the armhole curve ((3)-(5)). This will determine the depth of your sleeve head. Now draw in the curve of the sleeve head. It should measure 2 or 3 cm more than the armhole.

10. Draw in wrist measurement at the desired sleeve length.

You have now drawn your basic pattern. Before using it to knit a sweater, you should decide on a finished length for your sweater and draw in the depth of rib you would like at the hem and cuff. Trace the pattern onto a length of Tracing Roll and you are now ready to knit your sweater using the knitradar. If you don't own the full-width KR7 knitradar, you must trace only half the pattern onto your length of Tracing Roll.

ADAPTING YOUR BASIC PATTERN

Now that you have your basic pattern, you can use it as a starting point to make many more different patterns. To make patterns successfully, two things are necessary. The first is logical thinking – there is very little magic involved in the making of knitting patterns, just a little thought about what you're doing and why. The second is experience – you will, of course, only gain this by making patterns and knitting them, so don't be too ambitious to begin with. Keep detailed notes about each garment you make, including comments on how you could have improved it or which aspects were particularly successful. This way you'll rapidly build a source of reference and be able to draw on previous experience quickly and easily.

Basic front and back patterns.

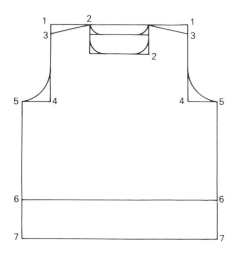

Basic sleeve pattern.

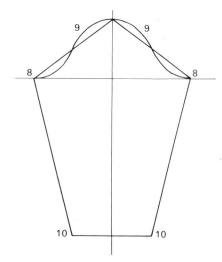

You will be able to see from the diagrams and notes that follow, how you can adapt your basic pattern by applying what you have already learned in this chapter and a little logical thinking. The dotted line on the diagram shows where the pattern has been altered. Rub out the old lines and any lines you don't need such as the waist line.

1. V-Neck Sleeveless Pullover

Decide how deep you want your V opening and draw in the new neckline. Don't forget to allow for

Cardigan with pockets.

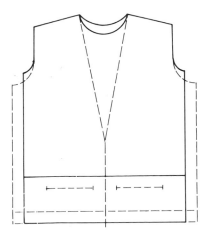

V-neck sleeveless pullover.

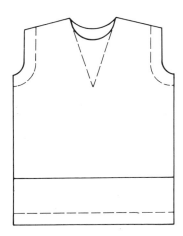

the fact that you will be reducing the depth by adding a neckband. The shoulder line has been made narrower and the armhole deeper to allow for adding a rib. A little extra depth has been added to the armhole to allow for the slightly looser fit which is normal on sleeveless pullovers. Decide on the length and draw in the rib.

2. Cardigan with Pockets
You will probably want a cardigan to be a looser fit than your basic pattern. Lower the armhole and

add to the bust measurement. Since you now have a larger armhole curve measurement, you should draw a new sleeve pattern using the method given for drawing the basic sleeve pattern.

Draw in the shape of the centre front opening, deciding whether you want the traditional neckline shown on the diagram or a crew neck. Although you will be adding some kind of band to the front opening, don't allow for it on your pattern. A little extra measurement on the front of your cardigan will help since your body also has a little extra at the front!

Using your tape measure in front of a mirror, decide where you want the pocket openings and mark them on the pattern.

3. Dropped Shoulder Sweater with V-Back
Continue the slope of the shoulder to make the sleeve. When drawing in the sleeve length, remember to measure from the shoulder point of your basic pattern, not from the new shoulder point. When you come to trace this pattern on to your knitradar paper, note that the continued shoulder line is the centre of the sleeve so you must repeat the same shape on the other side of this line to give you a complete sleeve. The top of the sleeve will be pointed giving a longer overarm measurement than underarm.

Decide on the depth of V you want at the back and make a slightly wider neckline if you like. Remember to use the front neck depth and not the back or you will end up with a very strange fitting garment. Most people don't realise that your neck doesn't come out of the top of your body, but out of the front of your body – hence the reason for deeper front necks than back necks.

4. Batwing Sweater with Slashed Neck
Use your tape measure in front of a mirror to decide how deep you want the batwing and how long the sweater should be. You can also gauge how wide to make the neck opening using your tape measure. You should lower the front neck a little and then compare the complete neck circumference with the neck circumference of your basic pattern. If your new measurement is smaller, then lower the front

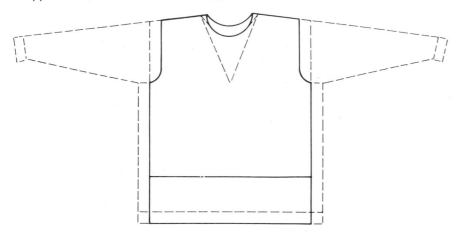

Dropped shoulder sweater with V-back.

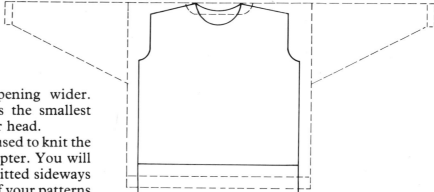

Batwing sweater with slashed neck.

neck some more or make the opening wider. Remember, your basic pattern has the smallest measurement that will go over your head.

A similar pattern to this has been used to knit the beautiful angora sweater in this chapter. You will notice that the sleeves have been knitted sideways rather than from the cuff up. Most of your patterns can be knitted sideways, simply by tracing them on to your pattern paper that way. If you don't own the full-width KR7 knitradar then you should draw in a centre line, trace one half on to your pattern paper, then trace the other half using a different colour of pencil. That way you will find it easier to identify which side of your knitting you should be shaping.

These four examples of adapting your basic pattern should give you enough general theory about making your own patterns to start you on the road to becoming a skilful maker of knitting patterns. As you will have seen, much of it is quite logical and straightforward if you take the time to think carefully about what you are doing and why.

CALCULATING THE NUMBERS OF NEEDLES AND ROWS REQUIRED

This can easily be done without the help of special gauges, charting devices or computers.

First prepare a good-sized swatch in the chosen yarn, stitch and colour to enable you to take a tension measurement 10cm (4″) square. Remember to allow your swatch to rest for an hour or more after taking it off the machine and before pressing or steaming. Mark the 10cm (4″) square with pins and count the number of stitches across the fabric and the number of rows deep. Now you need to divide the measurements on your drawn design by 10cm (4") and multiply by the number of stitches or rows accordingly. To make these calculations a great deal easier we have provided a simple chart to follow on pages 78–9.

Your next mathematical problem comes in working out the punchcard or relevant pattern repeat. A *few* extra stitches or rows will make little difference to the garment fit, but could help your design match up at the seams better. Again, the simpler the shape the fewer problems you'll have.

Charts to find the number of needles or rows required are on pages 78–9.

CALCULATING INCREASES AND DECREASES

Using graph paper to help you calculate where to increase or decrease is a lot simpler than the mathematical process. Having worked out the number of rows and stitches for the measurements of your design, you need to transfer these onto graph paper. It is usual to let one stitch represent one square on the graph paper, but, because a stitch is rarely square, your design may look a little elongated. This also needs to be taken into consideration when planning a picture motif or design on ordinary graph paper. What looks right on the paper will be foreshortened when knitted.

Draw in any curves as required and then 'square off' as close to the line as possible, as shown in the diagram. Although you will want both sides of your garment to match, remember how and when you can increase or decrease on your machine. For example if you can only increase a stitch when the carriage is on that side you will need to make the 'step' on your graph on even rows on the right side and odd rows on the left.

CALCULATING YARN QUANTITIES

There really is no way of accurately calculating how much yarn a garment will take. The easiest way to assess an approximate amount is to knit up a 25 or 50 gram ball in the required stitch, then calculate how many square centimetres (inches) one ball covers and therefore how many balls would be required to cover the total area of your design. Always approximate in excess – so add one ball to the figure you arrive at. You can always unravel the ball you've knitted up but do make sure that you knit your garment all in one dye lot.

After a garment has been knitted, an easy way of checking the amount of yarn used (especially if a cone was used) is to weigh the garment.

With a multi-coloured design you can expect a fair amount of yarn wastage but, as any keen designer will tell you, every odd ball comes in handy for experimenting with new ideas and swatches.

DESIGN BY COMPUTER

It is possible to use your home computer to calculate the instructions for designing and creating garments, the instructions can even be printed out for the knitter's use. Many professional knitters keep their instructions on floppy disc nowadays. Companies often display at knitting exhibitions so visits to these events can be informative as well as giving you lots of ideas.

ANGORA SWEATER BY KNITMASTER

Photograph on page 69.

For Knitmaster Chunky 155 and 150 machines with Knitradar and ribbing attachment.

The KR7 full width radar comes into its own when knitting asymmetrical patterns such as this, where the information for knitting one side of the garment differs from the other. Knitters with half width knitradar should use coloured pencils when drawing the pattern to identify to which side of centre 0 each line refers. This diagram is shown in one size to fit 81 to 86 bust. Use it as a guide line to draw the size you want to knit.

MATERIALS: 18 × 20g balls of Sandy Black Angora in white (col 1), 3 balls in khaki (col 2); 1 × 25gr ball of Twilleys Goldfingering (col 3).

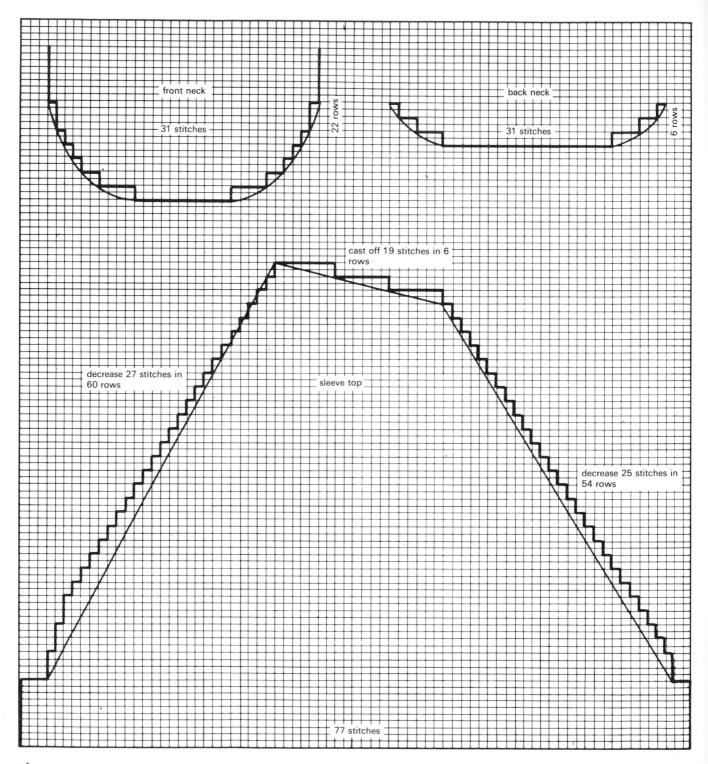

front neck

31 stitches

22 rows

back neck

31 stitches

6 rows

cast off 19 stitches in 6 rows

decrease 27 stitches in 60 rows

sleeve top

decrease 25 stitches in 54 rows

77 stitches

MEASUREMENTS: To fit 81 to 86cm bust; length 60cm; sleeve seam 48cm.

TENSION: 21 sts and 24 rows to 10cm over st st. TD approx 0. 20 rows to 10cm over 1/1 rib. TD approx R.

NOTE: The coloured 'Dart' sections are knitted by pushing needles into HP. After each colour is knitted in a dart, finish it with 1 plain row before starting next colour.

BACK and FRONT (alike)

Using col 1 cast on and K the required no of rows in 1/1 rib. Transfer sts to main bed and cont as instructed on radar.

SLEEVES

Knit one sleeve with dart and one sleeve plain. Using col 1, cast on and K 2 rows. Cont as instructed on radar, then finish with 2 rows in A. Cast off.

CUFFS

Using col 1 cast on and K the required no of rows in 1/1 rib. Transfer sts to main bed. With wrong side of sleeve facing pick up sts along cuff edge and put on to needles. Set TD to 5 and K 1 row. Cast off.

NECKBAND

Using M cast on and K the required no of rows in 1/1 rib. Transfer sts to main bed. K 1 row, then cast off.

TO MAKE UP

Pin out and press according to instructions in ball band. Join shoulder seams. Sew in sleeves between marked points. Join side and sleeve seams. Sew on neckband, fold in half to inside and sl st. Press seams.

Angora sweater (measurements in cm).

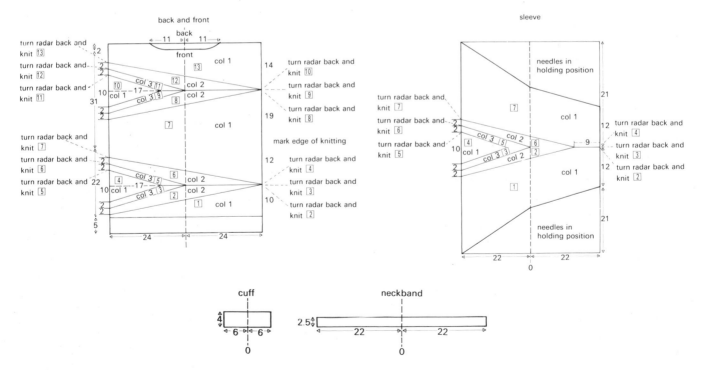

Squaring off to create curves.

Charts to Find the Number of Needles or Rows Required

Tension (total number of stitches *or* rows in 10cm)	1 cm	2 cm	3 cm	4 cm	5 cm	6 cm	7 cm	8 cm	9 cm	10 cm	20 cm	30 cm	40 cm	50 cm	60 cm	70 cm	80 cm	90 cm
							Garment measurements in metric											
10	1	2	3	4	5	6	7	8	9	10	20	30	40	50	60	70	80	90
11	1	3	4	5	6	7	8	9	10	11	22	33	44	55	66	77	88	99
12	2	3	4	5	6	8	9	10	11	12	24	36	48	60	72	84	96	108
13	2	3	4	6	7	8	9	11	12	13	26	39	52	65	78	91	104	117
14	2	3	5	6	7	9	10	12	13	14	28	42	56	70	84	98	112	126
15	2	3	5	6	8	9	11	12	14	15	30	45	60	75	90	105	120	135
16	2	3	5	7	8	10	11	13	15	16	32	48	64	80	96	112	128	144
17	2	4	5	7	9	10	12	14	16	17	34	51	68	85	102	119	136	153
18	2	4	6	7	9	11	13	15	16	18	36	54	72	90	108	126	144	162
19	2	4	6	8	10	12	14	15	17	19	38	57	76	95	114	133	152	171
20	2	4	6	8	10	12	14	16	18	20	40	60	80	100	120	140	160	180
21	2	4	6	9	11	13	15	17	19	21	42	63	84	105	126	147	168	189
22	2	5	7	9	11	13	16	18	20	22	44	66	88	110	132	154	176	198
23	2	5	7	9	12	14	16	19	21	23	46	69	92	115	138	161	184	207
24	3	5	7	10	12	15	17	19	22	24	48	72	96	120	144	168	192	216
25	3	5	8	10	13	15	18	20	23	25	50	75	100	125	150	175	200	225
26	3	5	8	10	13	16	18	21	23	26	52	78	104	130	156	182	208	234
27	3	5	8	11	14	16	19	22	24	27	54	81	108	135	162	189	216	243
28	3	6	8	11	14	17	20	22	25	28	56	84	112	140	168	196	224	252
29	3	6	9	12	15	17	20	23	26	29	58	87	116	145	174	203	232	261
30	3	6	9	12	15	18	21	24	27	30	60	90	120	150	180	210	240	270
31	3	6	9	12	16	19	22	25	28	31	62	93	124	155	186	217	248	279
32	3	6	10	13	16	19	22	26	29	32	64	96	128	160	192	224	256	288
33	3	7	10	13	17	20	23	26	30	33	66	99	132	165	198	231	264	297
34	3	7	10	14	17	20	24	27	30	34	68	102	136	170	204	238	272	306
35	4	7	11	14	18	21	25	28	32	35	70	105	140	175	210	245	280	315
36	4	7	11	14	18	22	25	29	32	36	72	108	144	180	216	252	288	324
37	4	7	11	15	19	22	26	30	33	37	74	111	148	185	222	259	296	333
38	4	8	11	15	19	23	27	30	34	38	76	114	152	190	228	266	304	342
39	4	8	12	16	20	23	27	31	35	39	78	117	156	195	234	273	312	351
40	4	8	12	16	20	24	28	32	36	40	80	120	160	200	240	280	320	360
41	4	8	12	16	21	25	29	33	37	41	82	123	164	205	246	287	328	369
42	4	8	13	17	21	25	29	34	38	42	84	126	168	210	252	294	336	378
43	4	9	13	17	22	26	30	34	39	43	86	129	172	215	258	301	344	387
44	4	9	13	18	22	26	31	35	40	44	86	132	176	220	264	308	352	396
45	5	9	14	18	23	27	32	36	41	45	90	135	180	225	270	315	360	405
46	5	9	14	18	23	28	32	37	41	46	92	138	184	230	276	322	368	414
47	5	9	14	19	24	28	33	38	42	47	94	141	188	235	282	329	376	423
48	5	10	14	19	24	29	34	38	43	48	96	144	192	240	288	336	384	432
49	5	10	15	20	25	29	34	39	44	49	98	147	196	245	294	343	392	441
50	5	10	15	20	25	30	35	40	45	50	100	150	200	250	300	350	400	450

Tension (total number of stitches *or* rows in 4in)	$\frac{1}{4}$ in	$\frac{1}{2}$ in	$\frac{3}{4}$ in	1 in	2 in	3 in	4 in	5 in	6 in	7 in	8 in	9 in	10 in	11 in	12 in	24 in	36 in
	Garment measurements in imperial																
10	1	2	2	3	5	8	10	13	15	18	20	23	25	28	30	60	90
11	1	2	2	3	6	9	11	14	17	20	22	25	28	31	33	66	99
12	1	2	3	3	6	9	12	15	18	21	24	27	30	33	36	72	108
13	1	2	3	4	7	10	13	17	20	23	26	30	33	36	39	78	117
14	1	2	3	4	7	11	14	18	21	25	28	32	35	39	42	84	126
15	1	2	3	4	8	11	15	19	23	26	30	34	38	41	45	90	135
16	1	2	3	4	8	12	16	20	24	28	32	36	40	44	48	96	144
17	1	2	3	4	9	13	17	21	26	30	34	38	43	47	51	102	153
18	1	2	4	5	9	14	18	23	27	32	36	41	45	50	54	108	162
19	1	3	4	5	10	15	19	24	29	33	38	43	48	52	57	114	171
20	1	3	4	5	10	15	20	25	30	35	40	45	50	55	60	120	180
21	1	3	4	5	11	16	21	26	32	37	42	47	53	58	63	126	189
22	1	3	4	6	11	17	22	28	33	39	44	50	55	61	66	132	198
23	2	3	4	6	12	17	23	29	35	40	46	52	58	63	69	138	207
24	2	3	5	6	12	18	24	30	36	42	48	54	60	66	72	144	216
25	2	3	5	6	13	19	25	31	38	44	50	56	63	69	75	150	225
26	2	3	5	7	13	20	26	33	39	46	52	59	65	72	78	156	234
27	2	3	5	7	14	20	27	34	41	47	54	61	68	74	81	162	243
28	2	4	5	7	14	21	28	35	42	49	56	63	70	77	84	168	252
29	2	4	5	7	15	22	29	36	44	51	58	65	73	80	87	174	261
30	2	4	6	8	15	23	30	38	45	53	60	68	75	83	90	180	270
31	2	4	6	8	16	23	31	39	47	54	62	70	78	85	93	186	279
32	2	4	6	8	16	24	32	40	48	56	64	72	80	88	96	192	288
33	2	4	6	8	17	25	33	41	50	58	66	74	83	91	99	198	297
34	2	4	6	9	17	26	34	43	51	60	68	77	85	94	102	204	306
35	2	4	7	9	18	26	35	44	53	61	70	79	88	96	105	210	315
36	2	5	7	9	18	27	36	45	54	63	72	81	90	99	108	216	324
37	2	5	7	9	19	28	37	46	56	65	74	83	93	102	111	222	333
38	2	5	7	10	19	29	38	48	57	67	76	86	95	105	114	228	342
39	2	5	7	10	20	29	39	49	59	68	78	88	98	107	117	234	351
40	3	5	8	10	20	30	40	50	60	70	80	90	100	110	120	240	360
41	3	5	8	10	21	31	41	51	62	72	82	92	103	113	123	246	369
42	3	5	8	11	21	32	42	53	63	74	84	95	105	116	126	252	378
43	3	5	8	11	22	32	43	54	65	75	86	97	108	118	129	258	387
44	3	6	8	11	22	33	44	55	66	77	88	99	110	121	132	264	396
45	3	6	8	11	23	34	45	56	68	79	90	101	113	124	135	270	405
46	3	6	9	11	23	35	46	58	69	81	92	104	115	127	138	276	414
47	3	6	9	12	24	35	47	59	71	82	94	106	118	129	141	282	423
48	3	6	9	12	24	36	48	60	72	84	96	108	120	132	144	288	432
49	3	6	9	12	25	37	49	61	74	86	98	110	123	135	147	294	441
50	3	6	9	13	25	38	50	63	75	88	100	113	125	138	150	300	450

CHAPTER 7
Cut and Sew

If you are a dressmaker as well as a knitter you'll enjoy being able to create your own knitted fabrics ready for sewing. The cut and sew method enables you to use your knitted fabric to make up more tailored-looking outfits without the restrictions and complications of shaping and finishing of a fully fashioned garment.

The outfit featured was made up from Vogue patterns but if you're a dedicated designer there is no reason why you shouldn't make up your own pattern and fabric. Then you really can say 'it's all my own work!'. You could even spin your own yarn – but that's another book! However, for the best results and most professional finish, here are some valuable tips.

Choose a pattern with the minimum number of seams – a knitted fabric is used to its best advantage on simple straight shapes avoiding darts.

Consider the maximum width of fabric you are able to produce on your machine and if the pattern pieces will fit without additional seaming or grafting. Do a stitch sample in the chosen yarn to determine this first. Jackets and coats frequently place the centre back pattern piece to a fold. It may be necessary to make a seam here for example.

Choose a yarn with at least 50 per cent natural fibre content and work it to the recommended tension.

You could knit your fabric by the metre on the full width of your machine but to avoid unnecessary wastage it's advisable to knit each pattern piece individually as much as possible i.e. a length a fraction wider and longer.

Press or steam the fabric, taking care not to destroy the natural bounce and texture of the yarn. Use a patting up and down movement, never slide the iron.

The rest is plain sailing – or rather dressmaking – I would like to recommend, though, that a stretch stitch be used for all seams, and edges are overlocked or zig-zag stitched.

Vilene can aid perfection and answer many a cut and sew problem, in particular with their Supershape and Fold-A-Band. Supershape is a unique interfacing which has definite advantages for the cut and sew enthusiast. Instantly recognised by a definite grain line, Supershape gives a professional finish to a variety of garments from coats to blouses. Applied correctly (it is ironed to the reverse side of the fabric) the knitting will not unravel or sag. It can also be used as a tape to stop seams stretching.

Fold-A-Band is an iron-on band that sets your sewing straight. It works particularly well for knitted fabrics ensuring a perfectly straight fold in details such as pleats, pocket tops, hemlines, sleeve edges, behind button holes, zips and openings. 'Firm' Fold-A-Band is ideal for waistbands.

CUT AND SEW SUIT BY JONES/BROTHER

Photograph on page 68.

SKIRT

MATERIALS: 300g of Yeomans Elsa. Waist length of elastic.

MEASUREMENTS: To fit 91cm hips; length 68cm.

TENSION: 27 sts and 40 rows to 10cm over st st.

Note: Skirt is worked in one piece from side to side. Push 197 needles into WP.

Using waste yarn cast on and K a few rows. COR. Break off waste yarn, join in main colour, set TD to MT. RC 000. Set for partial knitting. K 2 rows.** [Push 20 needles at left into HP, K 2 rows] 3 times, [push next 18 needles at left into HP, K 2 rows] 4 times, [push next 13 needles at left into HP, K 2 rows] 4 times. 13 needles now remain in HP. Push all needles back into WP and K 2 rows. (RC 26). Push 184 needles at left into HP, K 2 rows. (Push 13 needles at right back into WP, K 2 rows) 4 times, [push next 18 needles back into WP, K 2 rows] 4 times, [push next 20 needles back into WP, K 2 rows] 3 times. All needles are now back in WP. K 12 rows. ** RC 62.

Rep from ** to ** 19 times more. Using waste yarn, K a few rows and take off machine.

TO MAKE UP

Note that P side of work is the right side. Press work lightly according to instructions on cone. Take out waste yarn and graft cast on and cast off edges. Turn up 2cm hem at lower edge and sl st. Turn over 2.5cm at top and sl st, threading elastic through hem. Press lightly.

TOP AND COAT

FABRIC FOR TOP

MATERIALS: 1 × 3000g cone plus 50g of Yeomans Elsa.

TENSION: 21 sts and 51 rows to 10cm over tuck patt.

Card used was card 9 from Jones/Brother basic 840 set, but any suitable tuck stitch card can be used. Push 170 needles into WP. Cast on by hand. Set TD to MT, RC 000 and set machine for tuck stitch. K 3,000 rows or until work measures approx 6 metres, Cast off.

FABRIC FOR COAT (Worked on a Chunky machine with Intarsia facility)

MATERIALS: 26 × 25g balls of Emu Butterfly, 22 × 25g balls of Emu Filigree.

TENSION: 16 sts and 23 rows to 10cm over st st.

Push 104 needles into WP. Cast on by hand. Set TD to MT, RC 000. Work in Intarsia throughout, working squares of 26 sts and 38 rows and alternating the colours. K to RC 1064. K 2 rows plain. Cast off.

CHAPTER 8

Machine, Spinners and Designers

WHICH MACHINE FOR YOU?

The kind of machine you choose for yourself depends greatly on how much and what kind of knitting you intend to do. Are you, for example, going to specialise in the hand-knit look? If so the Bond or one of the chunky machines is the obvious choice. If you are intending doing a fair amount of work on your machine, or setting up a small business, a ribber or double bed will speed up welts and give more options for designing. And, on anything other than perhaps a chunky, a punchcard or alternative patterning device is a must for creative knitting.

The ultimate machine is, of course, the electronic. But they are not cheap and you need to be sure you can make good use of one – you could buy a lot of woollies for that price! The cheapest machine on the market is the Bond which is not so much a machine but an aid to speedier hand knitting. It's ideal for those who just want to make limited numbers but not so practical for mass production as it's much slower and involves more handwork than other (considerably more expensive) machines.

Before buying any machine take time to visit all the showrooms and try them all – one person's dream-machine is another's nightmare. Think about the type of work you want to produce – do you want intarsia or lace facilities or can most of your work be done by automatic patterning? Perhaps a reversible or circular fabric fits your design ideas, in which case you'll need a double bed. Don't be tempted to rush out and break the piggy bank on a machine that does everything just because 'one day' you might like to...! (Do you, for example, like me, have a sewing machine that does a 101 different embroidery stitches which has only ever been used for the straight and plain zig-zag stitches?). A modular system (like that offered by Pfaff/Passap) is possibly the ideal, whereby you can buy a basic machine and add accessories as and when you want (or can afford) them. The only draw-back here is that it ultimately costs quite a bit more than buying the machine complete in the first instance.

Here is a brief guide to some of the machines available and their accessories, but they all vary so much that they need to be seen, tried and tested before making up your mind.

KNOW YOUR MACHINE

A knitting machine is of no use unless you know how to use it properly and can make it produce what you want. I've lost count of the number of people who have told me about their 'old machine under the bed that never got further than two rows before it cast itself off'. IT IS MOST IMPORTANT TO HAVE GOOD TUITION. Most good retailers will arrange this for you when you purchase a machine and some companies produce sound tapes to accompany their instruction books – these are excellent. But if you have acquired a second-hand machine or have not been able, for some reason or other, to master your machine, DON'T PUT IT BACK UNDER THE BED! Try and contact the manufacturer or their agent to find out what courses of tuition they run, make enquiries at your local knitting club or adult education centre, or write to one of the specialist machine knitting magazines for their advice. The Machine Knitting and Design Centre runs courses for all types of machine. Contact Kamalini Trentham, High Cross House, High Cross, Aldingham, Watford, Herts. Tel: 092 76 3095.

Brother Electroknit – electronic machine
Comes with lace carriage
Standard gauge needle bed – knits yarns up to a soft DK
60 stitch basic pattern repeat
Intarsia can be worked by hand
Further attachments:
    ribber
    single and double bed colour changers
    intarsia carriage
    transfer carriage
    garter carriage
    linker
    charting device – Knitleader KL116

Brother KH891
Comes with charting device (Knitleader) and lace carriage
Standard gauge needle bed – knits up to a soft DK
24 stitch basic pattern repeat
Intarsia can be worked by hand
Further attachments:
    single and double bed colour changers
    intarsia carriage
    transfer carriage
    garter carriage
    linker
    ribber

Brother KH260
Chunky gauge machine – knits up to heavy chunky and hairy yarns
24 stitch basic pattern repeat
Thread lace can be worked by main carriage
Further attachments:
    charting device (Knitleader)
Available soon:
    intarsia carriage and ribber

Brother KH230
Chunky gauge machine – knits up to heavy chunky and hairy yarns
Patterning by hand selection
Intarsia can by worked by hand
Lace can be worked by hand transfer
Further attachments:
    ribber
    charting device (Knitleader)

Knitmaster SK560 Electronic
Comes with lace carriage
Standard gauge needle bed
200 needles
Complete accessory box
Forty-five stitch patterns included
Five blank design cards
Full set of knitradar patterns
Instruction books
60 stitch basic pattern repeat (varies any number from 2-60)
Push buttons to:
    reverse pattern direction or colours
    double pattern lengthways
    double pattern widthways
    mirror repeat
    knit single bed patterns in jacquard
Motifs can be placed anywhere on needle bed
Two motifs can be knitted simultaneously
Pattern can be 'centred' anywhere on machine
Knits as standard:
    tuck
    slip
    weaving
    platting
    fair isle
    tuck lace
    transfer lace
    fashion lace
    punch lace
Accessories:
    ribber
    4-way colour changer
    SC3 linker
    weaving arm
    tuition cassette

Knitmaster 600K Standard Gauge Punchcard Machine

Complete accessory box
20 punchcards
Facility for adding knitradar
Standard gauge needle bed
200 needles
Instruction books
24 stitch pattern repeat
Knits motifs
Stitch patterns:
   tuck
   slip
   weaving
   platting
   fair isle
   tuck lace
   punch lace
   intarsia
Accessories:
   KR7 knitradar
   weaving arm
   transfer lace carriage
   ribber
   4-way colour changer
   SC3 linker
   tuition cassette

Knitmaster 700K Standard Gauge Punchcard Machine

Complete built-in accessory box
Built in knitradar
Full set of knitradar patterns
Standard gauge needle bed
200 needles
20 punchcards
Instruction books
24 stitch pattern repeat
Knits motifs
Stitch patterns:
   tuck
   slip
   weaving
   platting
   fair isle
   punch lace
   tuck lace
   intarsia
Accessories:
   transfer lace carriage
   ribber
   4-way colour changer
   SC3 linker
   weaving arm
   tuition cassette

Knitmaster Chunky 150

Complete accessory box
Facility for adding knitradar
Wide gauge needle bed
110 needles
Instruction book
Manual patterning system
Tuition cassettes
Knits as standard:
   tuck
   slip
   two-colour slip (fair isle)
   intarsia
Accessories:
   PS150 pattern selector (punchcard system to fit 150, complete with punchcards)
   KR-7 knitradar
   SR150 ribber

Knitmaster 155 Professional Chunky Punchcard Machine

Complete accessory box
Five punchcards supplied
Chunky gauge needle bed
110 needles
Instruction book
Facility for adding knitradar
12 stitch pattern repeat
Knits as standard:
   fair isle
   tuck
   slip
   weaving
   punch lace
   tuck lace

Accessories:
    SR-155 ribber
    KR7 knitradar
    AG-155 intarsia carriage
    tuition cassette

Knitmaster 370K Fine Gauge Punchcard Machine

Complete built-in accessory box
Built in knitradar
Full set of knitradar patterns
Fine gauge needle bed
250 needles
20 punchcards
Instruction books
30 stitch pattern repeat
Knits motifs
Stitch patterns:
    tuck
    slip
    weaving
    fair isle
    punch lace
    tuck lace
Accessories:
    Transfer lace carriage
    FRP70 ribber
    4-way colour changer
    Tuition cassette

Knitmaster 270K Fine Gauge Punchcard Machine

Complete accessory box
Facility for adding knitradar
Fine gauge needle bed
250 needles
20 punchcards
Instruction books
30 stitch pattern repeat
Knits motifs
Stitch patterns:
    tuck
    slip
    weaving
    fair isle
    punch lace

    tuck lace
Accessories:
    transfer lace carriage
    KR7 knitradar
    FRP70 ribber
    4-way colour changer
    weaving arm
    tuition cassette

Bond

An inexpensive, simple and lightweight knitting system. It weighs only 4lbs, is 40″ long with a bed of 100 chunky gauge needles.
Handwork is used for ribbing and all patterning including: fair isle, intarsia, lace, cables and bobbles etc. It will knit all the popular and fancy hand-knit yarns. An extension kit of 30 needles is available.

Passap and Pfaff Passap

Every duomatic machine in the Passap or Pfaff Passap range is designed as an 'add-on' modular system, every machine can be adapted step-by-step to the changing requirements of every knitter by adding accessories.
Duomatic 80 double-bed machine with its own stand and 2 colour changer.
'Pusher' patterning system gives unlimited scope for all manual patterns on single and double bed, including:
    fair isle
    tubular fair isle
    tuck stitch
    tubular tuck stitch
    fisherman's rib
    selected fisherman's rib
    slip stitch
    overknit
    honeycomb
    carpet stitch (pile)
    cable stitch
    long stitch
    intarsia
    fringes
    edgings
    racking patterns

drop stitch lace
aran effects
pin tucks
stocking stitch
true ribbing
Accessories:
    Deco punchcard system (for automatic patterning incl. lace and weaving effects)
    Form computor – charting device
    Colour – 4-colour changer
    Electra 3000 – motor
Transfer carriage:
    U70 transfers stitches from double bed to single
    U80 for knitting stocking stitch and other knit purl combinations

Toyota KS858

Single bed machine with punchcard and manual selection button patterning systems
Can be converted into double bed with Rib Knitter KR505
Simulknit feature gives a perfect reversible fabric to punchcard fair isle patterning.
Optional extras:
    intarsia carriage
    4-colour changer
    charting device (Knit Tracer)
    platting feeder unit
    pile knitter
    blank punchcards and pop-punch

THE KNITTING MACHINE COMPANIES

Brother International Europe
Shepley Street
Guide Bridge, Audenshaw
Manchester M34 5JD
061 330 0111

Bond Knitting Systems Ltd.
Unit 21, Bridge Street Mill
Bridge Street
Whitney
Oxford OX8 6YH
Whitney (0993) 76449

Knitmaster
39–45 Cowleaze Road
Kingston-Upon-Thames
Surrey KT2 6DT
01 546 2444

Passap
Bogod Machine Co. Ltd.
50–52 Great Sutton Street
London EC1 0DJ
01 253 1198

Pfaff (Passap)
Pfaff House
East Street
Leeds LS9 8EH
0532 450645

The Singer Company (UK) Ltd.
255 High Street
Guildford
Surrey GU1 3DH
0483 71144

Toyota
Aisin (UK) Ltd.
34 High Street
Bromley
Kent
01 460 8866

THE SPINNERS

Copley
The name Copley has been known to hand knitters for over 50 years and is synonymous with quality yarns at cost-conscious prices. From man-made fibres to 100 per cent pure new wool, Copley put the emphasis on mix and match colours and yarns for high fashion designs that everyone can afford. L. Copley–Smith & Sons Ltd; P.O. Box, Darlington, Co. Durham DL1 1YW. Tel: Darlington (0325) 460133 Ext. 248.

Emu
The wide range of yarns from Emu offer something for every taste and every type of garment. They are

all of the highest quality in a fantastic range of colours and have a high fashion appeal. There are yarns made from 100 per cent natural fibres like wool and cotton as well as mohairs and others using a mix of natural and man-made fibres.

Emu Wools Ltd., Leeds Road, Greengates, Bradford BD10 9TE. Tel: Bradford (0274) 612561.

Knitmaster Kone Yarn

Designed and developed specially for machine knitting, the Knitmaster Kone range comprises 2ply, 4ply and Aran in an excellent colour palette. Special fashion ranges of Kone yarn are also available and vary according to seasonal changes and fashion trends. For stockist information contact:

Knitmaster Ltd., 39-45 Cowleaze Road, Kingston-upon-Thames, Surrey KT2 6DT. Tel: 01 546 2444.

Naturally Beautiful

Naturally Beautiful specialises in top quality yarns in natural fibres with spectacular colour ranges. There are 15 different types of silk and silk mixtures some with colour ranges of over 75 colours. Cottons encompass even more different weights and mixtures – one with a palette of 150 colours. Plus there is a wide choice of linen and linen mixtures from silk and linen to wool and linen.

Naturally Beautiful Ltd., Main Street, Dent, Nr. Sedbergh, Cumbria. Tel. Dent (05875) 421.

Phildar

Phildar's extensive range of yarns are both high fashion whilst maintaining down-to-earth prices. Many of their yarns are suitable for machine knitters ranging from their pure wools through to evening yarns. Phildar yarns are available throughout the country. For further information please write to:

Phildar UK Ltd., 4 Gambrel Road, Westgate Industrial Estate, Northampton. Tel: Northampton (0604) 583111/6.

Pingouin

Pingouin has transformed the traditional image of knitting with regular introductions of new colour and new types of yarn. Pingouin knitting catalogues always meet the current fashion requirements. Pingouin is readily available throughout the UK, please write for a list of stockists to:

French Wools Ltd., 7-11 Lexington Street, London W1. Tel: 01 439 8891.

Robin

Robin's range of fashion, DK and baby yarns, renowned for hand knit quality, are proving increasingly popular with machine knitters. Some yarns such as Soft'n'Easy are in 100g balls for ease of use, and ever popular Landscape and Reward DK produce an excellent fabric.

Robin Wools Ltd., Rodin Mills, Idle, Bradford, W. Yorkshire BD10 9TE. Tel: Bradford (0274) 612561

Rowan

Rowan yarns have probably the largest range of natural fibre colours on cone for hand machine knitters. There are 150 shades in a Light Weight DK suitable for all machines, 56 shades of a wool mark 3 ply Botany, 24 shades of a 4 ply Fleck Tweed, 25 shades of Cabled Mercerised Cotton and 14 shades of a Fine Cotton Chenille. The yarns are widely used by many designer knitters, many of the shades being selected by Britain's leading knitwear designer, Kaffe Fassett. For stockists write or telephone Rowan Yarns Ltd. at: Green Lane Mill, Washpit, Holmfirth, W Yorkshire HD7 1RW. Tel: Holmfirth (0484) 686714/687374. Mail order supplies may be obtained from their main stockist in London: Colourway, 112a Westbourne Grove, London W2 5RU. Tel 01 229 1432.

Sandy Black

The range of Sandy Black yarns includes the supreme 100 per cent Angora in 15 colours, 100 per cent Wool Twist (13 colours), 100 per cent Cotton Fizz (9 colours) and 75 per cent mohair (16 colours). All available individually or specially

packaged with one of the exciting designs from her catalogue. Send sae and £1.50 (deductible from first order) for colour catalogue, yarn samples, list of stockists and mail order details to:
Dept M, Sandy Black Original Knits, 164 Abbey Street, London SE1 2AN. Tel: 01 237 4736.

Twilley

Twilleys are specialists in the development of cotton and fancy yarns designed to be hand or machine knitted or crocheted. They have concentrated on the production of cotton yarn and have been leaders in this field since the formation of the company in 1941.
H. G. Twilley, Roman Mill, Stamford, Lincolnshire PE9 1BG. Tel: Stamford (0780) 52661/4.

Wendy

Wendy Wools have always been in the forefront of fashion knitting yarns and aim to produce new shades and qualities to complement the changes in fashion trends. Wendy Wools have produced some of the most succesful fashion yarns which are available through their many local stockists throughout the country. For further information contact:
Wendy Wools, Gordon Mills, Netherfield Road, Guiseley, W. Yorkshire. Tel: Guiseley (0943) 72264.

Yeoman

Have a good range of yarns for the machine knitter in fashionable shades, making them popular with many well-known knitwear designers. For further information:
Tel: 0537 532351

The Designers

Betty Barnden
The Triffic Design Company Limited
9 Alfred Place
London WC1E 7EA   01-580-5404

Isabella Bonnage
3 Fairfax Road
Colchester
Essex   0206-563292

Sarah Dallas
4 Derby Street
Colne
Lancashire   0282 868484

Judy Dodson
Yummy Jummies
Maytrees
Barcombe Mills
Nr. Lewes
East Sussex   0273 400500

Vanda Ingham
Knit Knacks
Hosey Trees
Hosey Hill
Westerham
Kent   0959 64577

Susan Nutbeam
Jones and Brother
5 Dryden Street
Covent Garden
London WC2   01-240-2430

The Knitmaster Design Studio
39–45 Cowleaze Road
Kingston-upon-Thames
Surrey KT2 6DT   01-546-2444

Louise Parsons
57 Talbot Road
Highgate
London N6   01-340-8390

Julia Pines
9 Frederic Mews
Kinnerton Street
London SW1   01-245-9852

Steve Wright
45 Melbourne Grove
East Dulwich
London SE11   01-299-3164

INDEX